Love Lifted Me

The Story of Fannie Billingsley Cooley Sullivan

Written by Cheryl Gore Pollard

Love Lifted Me, Second Printing
©2014 by Fannie Billingsley Cooley Sullivan
As told to Cheryl Gore Pollard, writer
All Rights Reserved

All rights reserved. No part may be reproduced without written permission from Cheryl Gore Pollard.
This is written to the accuracy of the memory of Fannie Cooley Sullivan and in her 'voice'. Characters may or may not have had name changed and situations are written as facts are remembered. This book or parts thereof may not be reproduced in any form, stored in a retrieval system, or transmitted in any form by any means without prior written permission of Cheryl Gore Pollard, except as provided by United States of America copyright law.

Published by Dogtrot Publishers
w/Eleos Press.com
www.eleospress.com

Cover Photo by: Cheryl Gore Pollard
Interior Formatting: The Author's Mentor,
www.LittleRoniPublishers.com

ISBN 13: 978-0692286821

PUBLISHED IN THE UNITED STATES OF AMERICA

Dedication

This story is dedicated to my grandchildren, great-grandchildren, and great-great-grandchildren with all my love. This is to help you know who you are and where you came from and even after I am gone,
to know that your lives are filled with love.

And to all the people who urged me to write my story.

This is for you.

Preface

This is the story of one woman's faith and determination to be a Godly model for those around her. She has traveled coast to coast, thousands of miles and overcome innumerable obstacles and has grown in faith and knowledge every step of the way. She has known joys and heartaches, successes and failures, comfort and fear. In the many, many hours I have spent with her I have come to know that she is a woman who walks what she talks. She does not discriminate between races; she loves us all whether we are white or black, addicted, without food, shelter or clothing, poor or considered 'affluent'. With her story comes the hope that those who read it will realize that life is not worth living without love—love for all. That is the message of Jesus, as she said so many times. It is her mission to spread the love of Jesus that radiates through and from her. In our talking and working together I have come to realize that she has truly been successful and blessed. She spreads this blessing through witnessing wherever she goes.

This book is a testament to that.

~Cheryl

The book is based on facts as recalled by Miss Fannie. Some names have been changed for personal reasons.

Love Lifted Me

One

The last of the boxes are stacked inside the house, sitting in their respective rooms. I stand outside on the cement walk with my hands propped on my hips and look at the front of my latest home. Another move, I think. I sigh. I have many, many years behind me and half as many different dwellings.

This house is lovely. Bright red trim and a sturdy red swing adorn the white exterior. I shake my head. Wonder if this will be my last stop along my long journey.

I shuffle to the steps and slowly climb to the dappled shade skittering around on the porch. I'll make this house my 'memory house', I think, as I lower myself into the red swing. It will hold all the mementos of things I've seen and done through my eighty-three years. I settle down on the swing's seat and let the tips of my shoes push the porch boards just enough to begin swaying. It is relaxing; gently moving to and fro, to and fro. At this time of afternoon I realize cars have all but stopped whizzing along the street beside the yard. Children at school and folks at work. It is quiet. I look about and see new green leaves dressing spring trees in delicate lacy garments and yellow daffodils dancing together in bunches. A bird sings.

I shift my body to get more comfortable. The swing continues its slow rhythm. I lean back and close my eyes. The gentle swaying lulls me away from the house, away from unpacking. I cross my arms on my lap and rest my shoulder against the swing's chain. The bird sings again but I am no longer sitting in the swing hanging on the porch of the white house with red trim.

≈

It is fall in mid-east Alabama. The year is 1934 and the Great Depression has left its mark, but it's hard to tell the difference between good times and depression times when you've been born into a sharecropper's family and have to work the red dirt fields.

I am four years old— I am back in the three-room, grey-weathered wood house where my family lives. The kitchen is warm. I hear the fire popping in the fireplace and smell homemade bacon frying on the wood stove in the black iron skillet. I think of how mother's mother must have had it hard: we do, too, but my grandmother was a slave. We didn't talk about that much.

I remember our house was a log house sitting between Wedowee and Roanoke, Alabama, plopped down in what was just a village really, called Midway since it was located 'midway' between the two towns. When I looked outside the door I saw long dirt roads and rows and rows of turned red dirt in fields where we'd planted corn and the remains of stalks peeked from the dirt where they'd been turned under. I would see more houses much like ours: our neighbors. Where we lived must have been filled with people of God. They were good; all of them, black and white.

Our house was built much the same as all sharecroppers': a bedroom where mother and daddy and we girls slept and another across the hall where the boys slept. There was a kitchen and a porch. In the winter one of the older siblings had to get up in the freezing house and make the fire, no matter what.

The work was hard. Mother and daddy both had to go to the fields. We raised everything. Corn, cotton; we wouldn't go to town to buy food, we milked cows and worked mules.

An early photo believed to be my father and mother, Lincoln and me.

My big brother, Willie B., had been born crippled; had nubs for some fingers and toes. I remember my daddy telling me that when he was little mother took him to the fields even though she had to tote him. He'd sit or nap on a pallet underneath big shade trees at the edge of the fields while she picked cotton. When he got grown, he could do almost anything. He would work all the time- from fixing and tinkering on things around the house to hauling logs.

One time that comes alive in my memory is when my brothers are in the house one cool, crisp fall morning. I smell the sweet odor of fresh parched corn seeping through the smoky wisps curling from the wood heater in the kitchen. There is Booker T., Albert, and Willie B. picking up the hot crunchy kernels from where they'd piled them on the floor after they had been parched, and eating them. They're having

a good time. I can tell the parched corn is mighty good—hot, crunchy, and so tasty. They know I want some, but they are older and bigger: they won't let me have any---and I'm mad. I go over and stomp the corn and it scatters in all directions. They yell and jump up to get me.
 Mother comes in.

The memory becomes harsher now, and I grimace as I remember the scene.

 Mother never says a word, just comes in the kitchen and holds me by my arm so I can't move away and whips me.

That thought fades to the second and last memory I have of my mother.

 Daddy tells me my mother is gone. She fell, he says. He is sad and his face looks older. His eyes are watery and his voice trembles. I see him taking Mother's nicest Sunday go to meeting dress off the wooden knob hanging behind the door and drapes it over his arm. He turns and leaves without another word.
 Later we get dressed in our Sunday clothes and ride in an open-topped roadster along the dirt road, following the funeral truck where my mamma's coffin rests in the back. I realized even then that my family was special. Most of the dead were taken to the graveyard on the back of a wagon pulled by a bull.
 I learn that when Mother died, my little baby brother or sister did, too, so there were really two people riding along in the back of that truck on the way to their grave.
 My daddy loved her so much. He always said he'd never seen another woman like her and never would see another one like her. I don't think he ever did.

Love Lifted Me

As we roll along my child's mind races. I think about my family. My father's grandparents and how I never knew them---on either mother's or daddy's side. Already dead before I came along. Mother's mother was a slave who ended up in Tennessee.

I look across the car seat at one of my favorite uncles who came home for the funeral. Mamma had a brother, Herbert, but we called him Sonny. He was an exslave that came down through Virginia. I can't imagine the life he must have had.

We rumble and jolt along the dusty dirt road.

Uncle Sonny

I remember how Sonny would take time to come and see me and my two younger sisters, Virginia and Virgello. Every time he visited us he always gave us a quarter each—and that was a lot of money back then. He was a kind of hero to me.

The motor of that car kept chugging and the wheels kept turning in the dry red dust, eating up the miles to the graveyard.

Herbert, (Sonny), named my sisters, but not me. There

was a white lady who lived close by and was part of the group of sharecroppers, and she named me Fanny. I remember that when mother was lying in the coffin, it was too high for me to see inside and that same woman came and lifted me up so I could have one last look at my mother. Everybody who lived and worked around the plantation, as we called it, respected each other, helped each other, and worked together.

It was a sad day, riding along. Any other time I'd be tickled to death to ride in such a fine automobile.

The car rumbled down the dirt road and trails of dust followed, chasing us along. We sat in silence on the way to bury my mother.

And that is the last memory I have of mother. The bird sitting in the swaying limbs of the tree sings again, but I won't wake. Dreams keep pushing along as I sit in the red swing.

Two

New Mamma

A little after mother died daddy married again. Her name was Mary. I don't remember her much; she died, too, not long after they got married.

Through all this time, with set-backs and losses, Daddy was good to us and did what he thought best. We always had food and clothes. To me he was just daddy, but the women liked him. Sometimes he stayed out all night, but me and my sisters were safe as long as our brothers were there in the house with us.

I smile as I think of a joke the brothers played on daddy.

Not long after Mary died, daddy went out and hadn't come home all night long. Daylight was just coming over the hills and in the early daylight hours it was hard to see. My brothers decided to play a funny trick on him.

Mary's clothes were still in the house, nobody had gathered them up and given them away yet. My brothers got up real early and came up with a plan to dress a scarecrow in Mary's clothes and prop it up beside the very road that daddy would have to travel down on the way home.

They had a time of this, giggling and laughing as they fixed up that scarecrow and imagining what daddy would think when he saw 'Mary' all dressed up and standing there in the morning sun, waiting beside the road for him to come home! They'd really give daddy a good fright, they thought!

That was a happy time. I remember another time that started out as a happy time, but I almost got in trouble. Virginia and I had gone with my brothers to the woods to cut firewood. We weren't going to help, just tag along and get out of the house. It was cold and they built us a fire in a semi-cleared out spot so we could sit beside it and keep warm. While my brothers cut wood, Virginia and I stayed by the fire and built a little playhouse out of limbs and pine straw.

Our 'house' caught on fire. I remember we jumped around and hollered, "The house is on fire, the house is on fire!" My brothers came running and stomped the fire and beat it with pine limbs until it was out. A close call, but all ended well.

We had fun even though we were poor. I learned early that we didn't have to have lots of money to have fun and enjoy ourselves. Where God is, we can be assured of his faithfulness and know He will keep us in his arms.

Three

Alma

A lot happened when I was so very young: mother died, Mary and her dying and then daddy married Mary's sister, Alma. She became my step-mamma. She had a daughter that was a little older than us who came to live with us, too, and Alma never did treat us the same as she did her own. Her girl came ahead of us. We were told to call Alma mamma but my brothers never called her mamma, but "You Know". They were older and could get by with more than me and my younger sisters. It was funny to us because we had a dog named—'You Know'. When Alma heard the boys call her "You Know", she'd frown up and say, "I ain't no dog!" She got aggravated, but the boys had their fun.

My thoughts shifted and whirled. I thought about the time I was given away.

By that time, and with daddy marrying Alma, times became even harder with two more mouths to feed and more bodies to clothe. Daddy had to give us younger girls away so the family could get along better and not be so strapped for food and other needs. We didn't think much of it; lots of folks had to do what they had to just to get by and having their children go live with another couple was a logical answer that made living easier for everyone. Pressure and stress, economic and physical, at home was eased and the "adoptive" folks had a helper living with them. I ended up living in one house with a childless couple and my sisters went to another near-by couple.

We settled in and life went on.

There were times when I was able to go visit outside the house. My new 'daddy's' folks were the ones who took in my sisters and they had a radio, a 'big thing' back then since hardly anybody could afford a radio. When Joe Louis was fighting, my 'mamma' and 'daddy' gathered me up and we went over to listen to the fights. That was an exciting time, a good time, when we could cheer Joe Louis on.

Back then we had a separate school from the white children. I was barely old enough, still about six or seven, but after school I'd walk my little sisters back to their place to keep bigger kids from jumping on them. We were strangers around there in our new 'homes' and even though I was still a little girl myself, I felt like I had to take care of them. I wanted to spend some time with them, too. I missed them.

I remember the white children had a big covered truck that picked up their children and carried them to school, but we had to walk to ours. While we were walking to school, every time that white school truck passed, they'd throw stuff out the window at us, whatever they had, jeer to us, and call us niggers. We had to run to the ditch to get out of the way and not get hit. I decided that the next time that truck came by; we'd pick up some rocks and throw them at the bus.

We did.

One of the rocks went through a window, and the truck driver stopped the bus and stormed out to see who was behind that rock throwing. The kids walking with me were scared and pointed me out. I took off running. I had to get home---I was so scared. I didn't know what that big driver might do to me.

I found out that that afternoon when the school truck met the black children walking on their way home, the driver stopped and asked them where I lived. After he got the white children home, he drove on by my house. He told Miss Lizzie (whom I was living with) to whip me or he'd have me sent to 'reformatory' school. When he left she got me. I knew her whipping was just a 'whipping', she knew very well how I felt…but even after that whipping I still had that threat of 'reformatory' school hanging over my head, so I behaved when I was out and about from then on.

After that, when the white children's truck passed us on the way to school the children never called us names or threw stuff at us, and we never bothered them either. I don't know what that truck driver said or did, but he put a stop to that meanness from the children. Maybe he taught the white students a lesson, too.

I had been staying with the couple a while, my 'new mamma and daddy'. There were only two rooms in that house, a bedroom and a kitchen. I had to sleep in the bed with the man and woman. I called them mamma and daddy because back then we had to call them that when we got took in.

One night I got roughly awakened. I was sleepy and thought I might be having a bad dream. I realized it wasn't a dream; the man was on top of me, jiggling, grabbing me, pushing and moving around. I could hardly breathe or move and I was scared out of my mind. What was he doing? I couldn't make a sound above a whimper. I didn't know what was going on… I squinted my eyes shut tight and blocked out my surroundings –

I couldn't look at him; I couldn't cry; I couldn't move. I was hurting something awful, then a ripping pain shot through my privates and I tried to put my legs together, but the man was there. There came a sharper, pressing pain, and I felt the skin near my bottom tear. The scream got caught in my throat and I could only sob quietly. Something awful, hurtful and deeply wrong was happening. Then I gave up and lay stiff and tried to lie still. I grabbed the bed sheets with both hands and squeezed 'til my fingers hurt.

When he rolled off me, I could tell there was a lot of blood. I felt a warm stickiness between my thighs and smelled that bloody, sharp metallic scent. I hurt something awful. I was scared and didn't understand why I was in so much pain and the sheets so full of blood. I knew something awful had happened but didn't know what to say, how to say it, or who I could even tell. I just scrunched myself up in a little ball and lay there between the woman's still body on one side and a hard-panting man's body on the other. Tears puddled in my eyes and trailed across my cheeks, dripping down and wetting the soiled sheets. As the man turned to his side and his breathing eased, he simply fell asleep. I curled further into the tiniest, tightest ball I could and squeezed my arms around me tight and prayed that the hurt would go away.

His wife never made a move.

Finally the sun came peeping through the window; morning was the only thing that greeted me warmly. I got stiffly out of bed and went to wash. I could hardly move. It was days before the pain and soreness went away—a lifetime before the emotional pain eased.

The woman, "mamma", had to know something evil had happened; she cleaned up the mess, washed the bloody sheets, but never said a word. Why hadn't she helped me? She just went about her business as usual. I would look at her, pleading with my eyes for help, but she made me know with her returning hard looks for me to keep my mouth shut. So I was simply ignored.

I didn't know what to do but I knew my daddy would.

I remember standing at the window that faced the much traveled road in front of the house, watching everyone who passed by. I knew if I stood long enough I'd see someone I'd recognize who had been to my daddy's house to talk with him. One day Johnny Whatley came by. I ran out to meet him, stopped him, and begged him to tell daddy to come and get me. He must have known, somehow, that I was in trouble and that I was so afraid.

He went to my daddy, and he came and got me and carried me back home. He went and got Virginia and Virgello, too. The couple who had them wanted them to stay, but I couldn't face going home without them, so daddy gathered them up and we were finally back home---all together.

In the days and weeks after I tried to make my mind go blank when that painful memory popped in. I thought that maybe I could erase that time and pretend that night-terror never happened.

So I did.

I was so glad to leave that house. It was bittersweet, though, because I hated to leave the school I was attending while I lived there. Going to school there was one of the best things that ever happened to me.

Four

Miss Mary and School

Our learning wasn't in a real schoolhouse but was held in the Steve Mission Church, a Methodist church. My teacher was Miss Mary Market. She was from Birmingham. She was good, and educated, and she really and truly taught us. She didn't put up with any mischief and she kept strict discipline. She didn't whip, she punished. We had to stand in the corner. None of us wanted to let her down and go to the corner; we just wanted to please her and make her proud of us.

She always said to get the information in our heads; that remembering is the art of learning. When we remember it, she'd say, we'd have put it in our heads and we could pull it out whenever we needed it. I felt that she was telling that especially to me; just to me.

I remember those words, and they've helped me all the way from that day to this. Miss Mary was right. I know now as I look back that there were many times when I felt that God was talking to me; just to me, like Miss Mary did then.

She was the best teacher. We had special spelling bees, and we would stand and recite poems and lyrics from memory. She taught us about things other than reading, arithmetic, and such. Every Friday we had a field day and she'd train us to do somersaults and turn flips. We learned to play together; get along with each other and find the good things in each other. In a lot of ways she was ahead of her time, the way she taught us.

She'd always tell us that if you can just smile, your trouble will vanish like a bubble. I heard that somewhere in the Bible it says that when you smile is when you're closest to God. Believe me, those words got me through a lot of hard times. The influence I got there from Miss Mary is what maybe mother and my step-mammas didn't, or couldn't give, and is the very foundation that every child needs.

How fortunate and blessed I was to have had such a wonderful teacher.

My schooling changed after Mr. Whatley got daddy to come 'rescue' us. When I got back home we went to Shining Light, a Baptist church that was also where we went to school. We went there about two years, but I didn't enjoy it as much as the other school. That teacher wasn't nearly like Miss Mary who made learning fun and taught us that learning is important.

And…I'd started wetting the bed since I'd been violated, and when I went to school I smelled like pee. I was still just a little girl and I didn't know about cleaning myself much and my step-mom didn't make me clean up. We had water and soap at school and the teacher would let me clean up some there. It was a hard time.

We had to walk about five miles from home to school and sometimes we just didn't go. When it was so wintery cold, so far and so cold in our thin clothes, we'd get about half way there and Miss Fannie Mae Robinson would let us come in her house and warm up. Some days we'd just stay with her all day and then go home and pretend we'd been at school. Daddy never knew about us skipping school, but he sure found out if one of us got a whipping when we were there: we got a note sent home!

I learned early about the dangers of playing hooky and dropping out of school and not finishing my education. Later, I had a hard time getting back in and finishing school.
I try to tell my grandchildren and young folks to stay in school and finish while they're young.

After about two years at Shining Light, we were finally provided a bus to ride to Roanoke to school. I remember census being taken while I was in school there. My birthday is on February first and on the census at school in Roanoke, it said April seventh. So I have two birthdays!

My childhood continued to pass dreamily through my mind as I sat in the porch swing. Shadows lengthened and the air cooled as the sun played its way across the sky---and my thoughts ran on. . .

Five

Good-bye Alma!

I was about ten and the years had passed to the early 1940s, and me and Virginia had spent the summer with our Aunt Lou in Gadsden, Alabama. When it came time for us to get back home she wanted to keep us, have us live with her and her man, but I wouldn't stay; I wanted to go home. The man living with my aunt wanted to keep us there, too. I didn't like how he acted toward us (something coming through to me like it had from my former foster 'daddy'---- maybe I could sense this?) He seemed to be 'too close' to us girls, but maybe my aunt couldn't see it, and she still wanted us to stay with them. No amount of convincing could change my mind. I wanted to go home! I remember my aunt threatened me by saying she was going to tell daddy I was a whore.

I didn't care. I went home and brought Virginia with me.

Another emotional time came to memory. A time back at home. I was about eleven or twelve.

A while after that, daddy had stayed out all night again. Me and Virginia were in the kitchen cooking breakfast. Alma's daughter had gotten old enough to go off on her own, and she had, so we sisters had things most to ourselves at home.

One morning, we had spend-the-night company the night before and as soon as we got up, our girlfriend slipped over to our brother's bedroom. Virginia wanted me to tell Alma about it, but I wouldn't tell and Virginia and I were fussing about it while we fixed up the breakfast food.

Alma came in and told me to hush my mouth and stop that fussing or she would hit me over the head with a piece of stovewood. I let her know I wasn't going to mind her none, and I huffed a little and tossed my head kind of sassy. I didn't believe she'd hit me but what I did, acting so prissy, really made her mad. She reached over and picked up a piece of stove wood and hit me---hard---across the shoulder. It hurt and surprised me but when she hit, I grabbed at her, thinking she was really mad and probably would hit me again. I didn't get my hands on her but she grabbed me and wouldn't let me go; she had me good! She put her head down and bit me on my ear, nearly taking off the top, and then brought more blood when she bit me again beside my eye.

Virginia, dancing and hopping around out of her wits and shaking all over, started hollering for Albert, "Come in here and get this whore off Fannie!"

By the time Albert, who was in the barn shucking corn for the cows and mules, came running in the kitchen, Alma had come to realize she was in for it. She let me go and got her shoes on and was out of there before we could say 'squat'.

She ran to the woods. My brothers looked all over but never found her. I haven't seen her from that day to this, but have a couple of scars that remind me of her every time I look in the mirror.

Alma gone. Hard times come back visiting. Daddy said he had to give me away again.

I loved my daddy. I never stood up to him or back-talked

him, but this time I wasn't being given away. I vowed that the last time I had to go would be the last time and I meant it. I was so torn; the last thing I wanted to do was hurt my daddy. My heart ached and I was afraid. I feared living with strangers again and that fear overrode obeying daddy. I knew I had to stand up to him and it broke my heart.

He meant that I had to go… there was just no way I could stay at home anymore and everybody have what they needed to get by. I knew that woman he'd planned to send me to. I thought she was nasty; she dipped snuff. My mind was truly set in hard stone that I would not go to that house. Virginia and Verjello could go, but not me. With tears in my eyes, I told him that I would go away if I had to, but I would never come back home again to live. And I didn't.

I see here where God was working personally with me, even in the bad times. He looks after all of us in the bad times as well as in the good ones. I can say that I'm sorry for the way I talked to my daddy and for the wrongs I have done.

Six

Stepping Along God's Path

My older sisters, Rose and Ruby, lived and worked in Bowdon with the Minnifields. When they heard that I had to leave home, they sent for me to come babysit for the Minnifield children. God solved my problem!
So I moved to Bowdon.

Outside a car passes; I hardly hear it. A cool late breeze brushes by and makes me shiver. I return to the present.

≈

"Grandma!" I hear. My eyes open and I see my grandson coming up the walk for an afternoon visit. "What'cha doin' Grandma?" he asks. "You won't get that house fixed up sitting there in that swing. Need any help getting them boxes unpacked?"
I sigh. The whole afternoon had passed and I hadn't gotten one thing out of the boxes and put away. I had let my mind travel to times past and the clock ticked the afternoon away.
I tried to focus on the now. My mind, filled with of

memories that floated past like wisps of battered spider webs, made my thinking a little slow. I could still feel the hurt and disappointments of times I'd experienced in my early years; more hardships than lots of people face in most of their lives. I'd had to grow up fast. God had been with me, always then. He knew, even in those heartbreaking, sometimes terror-filled times, how I would need to draw on the strength and understanding hard times had taught me.

I watch my grandson, Tarrius, stepping along the walk. He comes alone, and I remember how I've always felt as if I had no one to 'compliment' me: I was an odd one out--alone. My brothers and sisters had each other—they were born by twos: Booker T. and Willie B., Ruby and Rose, Albert and Lincoln; and then came me, the odd one, and finally Virginia and Virgello. I was a single; only half of a pair. I had no sibling as a 'mate', confidant, or helper.

Another example of God's hands reaching down during 'his time' and putting me where I needed to be—even at birth. He needed me to be able to go out and work alone; to use me for His Glory.

I lived my formative years without the guidance and help of my mother, but was fortunate to have a wonderful teacher to help fill in where my mother's love and kind words were missing. I thought of the time I was so little and so alone and hurting so bad in that bad foster house. I had to rely on myself to stand still beside that window, wait and watch; search for someone to help me and get my father to bring me home.

Go find my father. Like a strike of lightning, it hit. All the time I was so small, so alone. I realize now that even as a small, lone child, I had a Father who looked after me. I didn't know him at that time, but in the depths of my heart, even then, I was looking for my Father; my Heavenly Father, to hold me and one day bring me home. And He had me close to Him all the while. I smiled and stood and stretched.

I motion to my eager grandson. "I'm ready to get started. Come on in and we can do what we can before dark." I put my arm around his shoulders. "Bet I can fix us up something good to eat for supper, too."

We walk together through the door and it shuts softly behind us as we walk together into the red-shuttered house.

Seven

The Minnifields

Later, after supper and my grandson had gone home, I begin opening boxes that we'd stacked in my bedroom. I come across a picture of Mrs. Mildred Minnifield. Ah, a good family, I think, as I recall my move back to Bowdon. This well-known black family had helped Rose and Ruby. I was fortunate to have been asked to become a part of their family, and I grew so close to them. I look at the aged photo and parts of the years I spent there swirled through and came to focus in my memory.

≈

I was twelve, and it was 1952 when I came to live with Jessie and Maggie Minnifield that last time daddy had to send me away. That time it was my older sisters who came to my rescue, so I didn't have to go somewhere and live with complete strangers.

There were four children in the Minnifield family, and I stayed in the same room with them. I was more like a big sister to the two boys and two girls. I looked after them and worked cleaning the house and did whatever Mrs. Minnifield asked me to. I lived there about two years and attended Hudson Elementary—now a cemetery.

Too bad the school is gone; a part of history, all gone.

I really did like living there. I got new clothes and shoes in a timely manner just like with the Minnifield children. We got along and I loved being in such a good place. It was so different from living back at home in that sharecropper field. I helped do anything Miss Minnifield needed me to do. I looked after the children and kept them on a regular routine just like she asked me to. I felt at home like I was part of their family.

Time passed quickly while I lived there. I was growing up.

And I was happy.

Eight

Learning to Learn

When I reached my early teens, my sister, Rose, married John Cooley, and I left the Minnifields and went to live with them. They lived on "the hill" across town from the Minnifields. There was plenty of time for work, little time for school. I couldn't worry about that, though. Just had to survive. I'd work for Miss Mildred in the morning and pick cotton in the afternoons. My school days ended.

We had church every other Sunday, alternating at different churches, and we'd walk to the churches on meeting days. Rose's daddy-in-law was a deacon at church. We all went to church together and I still got to see the Minnifields at Sunday service.

The grownups went to night church—we children had our church at home on those nights.

My life was filled with work and getting by. Miss Minnifield, the woman I'd helped with her children, worked for Miss Mildred Lipham, a school teacher at Bowdon High School, and her husband was the Bowdon Post Master. When Miss Minnifield left her job at Miss Lipham's and took another job seeing to housework for the Moores, a wonderful door of opportunity opened for me, and I started working Saturdays for Miss Lipham. She was a wise woman. She took time to talk with me and taught me so many things: how to cook and how to wait on a table and set it properly and do fancy things. She was an artist too. One of the most important things she taught me was to communicate.

My cooking and communication skills proved to be something valuable as I traveled later in my life. Later, how I used these things I learned from this wonderful woman. God had 'set in place' these opportunities from my early age to help me. He places us where we can learn and have experiences to support us along our travels in life.

Miss Lipham was a Sunday school teacher and a Brownie leader and let us all get together and have a good time. Many times when I was there at her house, I was the one to take care of the Cub Scout meetings if she had to stay late at school. I really learned lots of things when I did that---and felt proud when she trusted me with that responsibility.

She treated me like family and I loved her. I worked with her a lot and she was a good woman to me, almost like a big sister.

In the 1950s, Bowdon was a special place. There were people who accepted and embraced all people, and I came to begin to see for myself that society isn't about color, but more about the 'haves' and the 'have nots.' Poverty and hard times fall like a blanket and where it falls, it covers everyone, not just a particular group.

I thought about all this during the time I walked to work. I never took the shortcut through the alleys. I walked the long way around. To me, the long way was the safest way. I could see danger and avoid it as long as I walked in the open-the lighted way out of the dark shadows. The alley, like a lot of shortcuts, held dangers and obstacles that I might never see. It was worth a little more time and effort to get safely where I was going than taking a shortcut (risk) not getting there at all. If I watched where I was going and stayed out of the alleys maybe that poverty blanket wouldn't be so heavy on me.

I saw the news on TV at Miss Mildred's and knew about social unrest and how groups of people were beginning to work for changes. When I was home at Rose's, I heard whispers about the FBI, CIA, and even the Clan from neighbors and people who visited. These intimidations became a quiet, rippling band of fear that knotted in my stomach and stayed with me (and most others, too). We lived in fear as well as near poverty.

I also worked for the Cunningham family around that time. I remember Mr. Cunningham saying, "I want to ask you something. How can you blacks still laugh and go on when whites and others treat you so bad?"

I answered that whites were not doing that to me, the ones I were in contact with were good to me.

But I knew I was fortunate. Not all whites were like those I knew. And I knew, too, that not all blacks wanted to work hard to earn respect. I lived and walked on a fine line and it was easy to cross and act one way or the other.

Seems almost surreal now, but was a constant threatening fear in those times—a way of life.

While I was working for Miss Mildred, I saw on her television where President Truman was explaining about welfare, a program to help poor people. I knew families in Bowdon who lived in dire need and were barely getting by. I took a pair of gloves, (We'd heard all sorts of things concerning the FBI connected to Civil Rights and I was afraid they'd be able to identify me come after me by checking fingerprints left on the paper!) and typed letter on Mrs. Mildred's typewriter and mailed it off to President Truman. I wanted to learn more about this "welfare" and how people who needed help could get it. His aid wrote back (I couldn't imagine him knowing what address to send a letter to after all my precautions!) and told me where people could go to in Atlanta and get help. I got the information out. Families got some help. Due to the letter sent to the White House and my passion to help, Truman recognized my effort and sent <u>me</u> a check! I was surprised and thankful. I didn't know anywhere in town to get it cashed so I carried my check to a man we knew as The Goatman, a local man, Mr. William Harvell, to cash it. He was a friend and always good and helpful to me and to many others.

Mrs. Mildred Lipham who taught and encouraged me so much. This photo was taken on one of my trips home. I was calling to talk to her lovely (now adult) daughter.

I sat and sifted through another box. I found an old dress pattern. My thoughts flew to Mrs. Thomas.

During those years working as a domestic in Bowdon, other opportunities to learn about things I'd missed learning from my mother came along. Mrs. Thomas, the wife of Dr. Thomas, was probably one of the first black home demonstration agents and 4-H club advisors in the state, taught a group us how to sew and make our own clothes. Some of the girls modeled their dresses in front of the class. We had a fun time of learning how to better make do with the little we had.

We canned sausage and chickens. We'd cook them up and put them in jars and pour the hot grease over them. Then use hot lids to seal the jars. This provided really good eating later on. She let me conduct some class demonstrations after she taught us. It filled me with self-confidence and pride. And that was something I'd lost and really needed building back up.

My 'modeling' and demonstrations gave me my first cupful of confidence to speak in front of a group of people. God filled that cup to overflowing that I needed as I traveled my life's journey.

Mrs. Thomas was a great woman and powerful influence in my life. I'd always dreamed about going to school and becoming a teacher like her, Miss Lipham, and Miss Mary. Mrs. Thomas was another woman who encouraged me to be strong and follow my dreams.

I got up and walked to the hallway and placed the faded pattern in a special place on a shelf at my 'memory wall'. I had already arranged a display of mementos and photos on the hallway wall so I could see them and touch them every time I passed through.

They would be there for my children and grandchildren to see, too.

Nine

Pete

It's getting late, but I'm not tired. I pull out another box and as I sift through papers, I find Pete. He filled another part of my life. I look at his face in the faded photo and brush my fingertips across his lips. My heart is filled with broken love.

Not all of our time was hard times; we had plenty of good times, too.

I lean back in my chair, drop the photo into my lap, close my eyes and time whips back...

I was about fifteen, staying at my sister, Rose's house, working as I could, and had barely started seeing boys. I always wanted to get married and be a school teacher. That was my dream, so boys didn't fit in much at all.

I wasn't very knowledgeable about boys, didn't know how to protect myself from pregnancy, or what the monthly periods really were.

Sometimes while I was at Rose's the feeling of being 'alone' often washed over me like it had when I was a child; me being the odd sibling in our family. I felt the hurt of not being able to grow up with a supporting and loving mother and it pierced my heart. My sisters helped as they knew how but perhaps they thought I knew more about the facts of life than I really did and didn't need more guidance, or maybe they were simply struggling hard with their own families to think about having 'talks' with me.

I remember an older boy, a nice young man, who started coming by and taking me to the movies and was good to me. I felt grow-up when I was with him. Yet I still felt young enough to go outside and play ball and have fun on many Sunday afternoons. I was old enough to feel a special enjoyment during private times with this older boy, but still young enough to run and play and have a good time with my friends.

He was a nice person and very good looking. There was one time he convinced me to go out with him—just me and him. We went to a 'joint'---and I knew better and had a few qualms about going, but I really liked this boy and wanted to be with him. We left the 'joint' early and started walking back home. Along the way on the corner of the street was a place we called it a 'juke joint' where we stopped to get a Coke to drink. (Other kinds of drinks were available there, but I was too naive to know.)

While we were ordering, a Carrollton man was came up and leaned down between me and my date to reach something on the counter. My young man gave him a 'what do you mean?' look. I guess the Carrollton guy didn't like that look much. He suddenly reached over me toward my date and had a knife clinched in his fist! He swiped his arm over my shoulder, pushed me down, stretched out his arm and cut my friend! Before I knew what was happening, my handsome date came out with his own knife and got a slice in the Carrollton man. Oh, what had I gotten myself into?

The police came.

This was my lesson learned. One learned and remembered. I never went that route again. I never did become one to party, go to 'joints', or be someplace where I knew I shouldn't be in the first place. I still liked the older boy, in spite of the ruckus he got us into, but Virginia wanted to match me up with another boy, a younger one. She had a boy in mind for herself and had it figured out that it would be handy for us to double date.

I really liked my older choice for a boyfriend, but Virginia's pick for me was nice, too.

When Rose and her husband went to the movies, the boys, the ones Virginia liked, came by the house to see us. By then, I had all but given up on my older suitor and went along with my new beau.

And that's when it happened. I got pregnant when I was only fifteen. I didn't know what to do. I didn't tell the boy: we were just kids and what could he do to help me anyway?

I left my job with Mrs. Lipham, feeling disgraced, when I found out I was pregnant. I had joined the church when I was younger. I brought disgrace on my church family as well as my family when I got pregnant. "Good girls" did not find themselves in this predicament. I went and made acknowledgements to my church family and apologized to my family. I was so ashamed. I could barely face anyone. I wanted to run away and hide.

So I did.

I caught the bus and went to my cousin's house in Anniston, Alabama, and Booker T. came to meet me there. He paid for the midwife when it was time for my baby to come. There was no doctor and my son was born at the house. Back then new mammas had to stay in the bed for a week and could have no full baths. That was a mighty long week!

Booker T. always called my baby his son since he didn't have any children of his own. I named my son Lawrence and called him Larry. He turned out looking a lot like Booker T., too.

I didn't know what to do or how to care for a new baby. I breast fed him at night and fed him bottles with Pet milk during the day when I went to work at Anniston Laundry. He got sick. We finally took him to the doctor and the doctor changed his milk to Carnation. Larry got better then.

I was just a little over sixteen years old and had a baby to tend to and a job to keep up. Looking back, I guess my dream of becoming a teacher started fading about them. I couldn't go to school; other responsibilities weighed heavier. God was with me and gave me wisdom to set priorities. I wanted the best for my baby and for him to have a more stable childhood than I'd had.

We can't always control our circumstances, but we can use God's given wisdom to choose the path to take, and make good come from the times we've acted without thoughts of what consequences might follow.

I didn't know any way to live but to work to make a living for me and my baby. I'd had some good women in my life who taught me to keep on going; work hard, do what I could to hold my head up and take care of my child.

When my son was about a year and half old, Rose, my sister back in Bowdon, got sick. She sent word that she wanted me to come home. She and her husband were farming and needed help. I went. I worked in the fields.

The times were much the same for all our neighbors and family around there: lots of people living in one house, hard work, little money, but finding time to relax and have a little fun. We thought about what other people were going through dealing with Civil Rights and were anxious to learn about how they were faring. But our lives there in Bowdon were wrapped up in our everyday concerns: making a living.

While Larry and I lived with Rose and her husband, John, I got to know his brother, Pete. He was a good-looking man and I needed to feel loved. I wanted the warmth and comfort of fitting in and having someone of my own. Then it happened again-another baby. I didn't want to face Pete (the baby's daddy) or my family. I was emotionally down; couldn't believe I was with child again but knew I had to stay strong. What other choice did I have?

Two babies and no husband; I was considered a whore and looked down on by the entire community. There were strict rules back then, especially for a woman with two fatherless children. I couldn't associate with many people at all. I wasn't allowed to be around anyone who didn't have children because I would be a 'bad influence' on them. I felt so low. I was ashamed and I was afraid. I had to leave again. Run away—my answer to my problems.

I didn't tell Pete about the baby. I didn't tell anybody—I just left. I took Larry and moved to Wedowee to Willie B.'s. He was married and they took me in. I stayed there until Wilma Jean was born. She was a good baby just like Larry had been. I remembered what I'd been taught when I lived and worked with Ms. Minnifield and Ms. Lipham. I put my children on a schedule. This kept them fed, rested, and comfortable, and I loved and cared for them. I wanted them to *know* that I loved them. The good families where I had worked and learned so much had molded me into being a loving and caring mother.

While I was in Wedowee with my babies the Minnifields moved to the country and their old house, which was in walking distance to the Lipham's, became empty.

The Liphams signed for me to get the house, and so it was arranged that me and my children could live in the old Minnifield home. I got the house for $600.00. A lot then, but God blessed me so we would have a good place to live. Oh, how God worked for me and my babies!

Finally the day came when I was able to get back to Bowdon in my 'new' home and go back to work for Mrs. Lipham. When I got there, I had to go back to the church and make acknowledgements again. God was working with me even then. I had the basics of living a good life and was trying hard to do the things I should. Sometimes what we want to be and how we want to live just doesn't happen the way it is in our dreams. I experienced shortcomings and sometimes I didn't know where to turn, but with God's guidance I never let any setbacks keep me down long. I learned to keep looking forward and hoping to have a good life—I had to be positive or depression would defeat me.

Even with the stigma of having two children out of wedlock, I still dreamed—I just changed a few details of what I'd planned my dream-life to be. I wanted to have a good, happy, full life and was ready and willing to work hard to make the dream of my future come true. I knew that sitting and waiting and hoping would bring zero results.

Because Pete and Rose's husband, John, were brothers, we were in company a lot when I visited Rose. They were all family. There were days when I helped and carried water to the fields when the men were working. Pete and I were together a lot. I came to really love him, not be simply infatuated with him, and I told him about the baby girl we had. He already knew all about my son, Larry, and during our lives together accepted him as his son and never treated him otherwise.

Pete and I married on January 12, 1952 and made our

home together in the Minnifield house.

As a young girl, I learned many hard lessons concerning 'living'. When I grew to know Pete, I grew to love him. He was a good, fun-loving man, in his own way, and taught me to be a good wife. I am thankful for my life with him, and for his role as my husband and being the father of my wonderful children.

Without him, there would be no 'them'.

Pete

We increased our family over the years, quickly. The years flew by and Pete and I had Willa, William (Eddie), James, (Jimmy named after Dr. Watts and his grandfather), and James (in the Bible), Frederick (Freddie, named after Dr.

Martin), and Timothy (Tim, from Timothy in the Bible). Tim's middle name is Allen, from a nurse I worked with. She wanted him to be named after her and I did. We never had any trouble naming our children, each one has a special name chosen by me and Pete that's perfect for them.

Pete's mom didn't like me, much ever. I guess she never really believed Pete was Jean's daddy, or maybe she just couldn't accept that I already had a child when Pete and I were married. Jean had light skin and my mother-in-law doubted she was Pete's—and didn't make little of it. She talked bad of me.

Pete's dad, Pappa Jim, was light skinned and always took up for me. He said, "Look at back of her head," and there was a birthmark. When he saw that he smiled and said, "She's a Cooley."

That put an end to my mother-in-law's bad mouthing, but she never did warm to me.

My eyes are tired. I'll rest now, I think, and open more boxes tomorrow. I put my special mementos that I want to display to one side and the others back in the box. At last I climb into my bed and pull my quilt over me. Sleep and rest and sweet dreams.

Ten

Nursing

Early today, just after breakfast, I get back to unpacking and open a small trunk. There are more papers, photos, mementos. I lift a yellowed photo of Bowdon Area Hospital and think of the times there. Oh, so much I learned!

When Pete and I first got married, I continued working for Mr. and Mrs. Lipham another two years at full time employment. Then I got a job at the hospital at night. I was no longer full-time with Mrs. Lipham, but I still cooked for her and could care for my children during the day.

I remember Mr. Lipham buying a dishwasher and telling me he didn't need me anymore. He was just joking—he always loved to carry on and joke. He did have a serious side, though. He told me we'd have a place to live and be helped, but if I got out there and acted like lots of folks did, he'd have nothing to do with me. I knew he meant that and knew he expected—and believed—me to be a good person.

While I worked at the hospital I was trained like a nurse, but I never got a certificate for it. The hospital wasn't integrated then, either, like schools weren't. Black people could be treated upstairs and have procedures conducted there, but had to stay for their extended care and treatment in rooms in the basement. Many times I saw black patients loaded in the ambulance from the upper door, driven around to the back of the hospital, and unloaded to a room in the lower area. Nurses, black and white, made a thousand steps a week going up and down those stars to treat their patients.

Nurses and I often talked about tragedy coming after midnight—and especially on weekends! Seemed that way at least since we saw our share of late night accidents.

I learned to do everything: give shots, baths, provide comfort, and tend to babies. And I 'caught' many of them as they dropped from their mammas!

I smiled as I remembered how I would feel the bellies of expectant mothers and predict whether they were having a boy or girl—no sonograms back then! I really had a gift...we really enjoyed sharing our ideas and predictions. Most of the time, my "feelings" and predictions were right!

I loved working with the people there. The Bible says the best teachers are self-experienced learners. When the nurse showed me how to give a shot, I tried to watch closely, but that wasn't like actually giving a shot. I remember when I had the opportunity to practice on Eddie and Jimmy. They were in the hospital and they cried when the regular nurses tried to give an injection. The nurse had to call me, and I learned to give shots through my experience giving them to my sons.

I sift through the box and find a photo of Jimmy . . . and a new memory burns behind my eyes.

One Saturday night Pete was going out. "Pete, can you ride with some of your friends tonight?" I asked. For some reason I had a feeling that he needed to leave the car; that I might need it. He said he wouldn't need the car and about that time I heard his buddy's car pull up in the front yard. He gave me a quick kiss on the cheek and went on with his friends.

I busied myself getting ready for bed and for church the next day: putting the freshly laundered sheets on the bed and laying out the children's clothes for Sunday services. I asked Jean to go in and make the bed for my sons. She came running back into my bedroom, screaming and crying, "Mama, come quick! Jimmy's in trouble!"

I dropped what I was doing and hurried past Jean to get to Jimmy. I reached his side and saw his eyes were rolled back in his head—I could only see white--and I knew I had to get him to the hospital.

"Larry!" I yelled, "Get the car!" Larry hit the door in a run and brought the car to the steps by the time I got Jimmy bundled up.

Larry had to become a man all too soon. He was the oldest and I relied on him very much. As I bundled Jimmy, my mind raced... Larry had always been my helper: even as a seven-year old, he'd get up early and fill the wood stove and cook breakfast before I went to work.

Strange thoughts I had as I rushed to get Jimmy to the car....

"Hurry, Larry," I called. Then to his sister, "Stay here, Jean," I told her, "and see to the others. Get them on to bed. I'll be back as soon as I can. And pray!"

I got Jimmy to the car and Larry rushed us to the nearby emergency room.

I stood back while the nurses began working on my little Jimmy. They bathed him in alcohol and tried to get in touch with Pete. He was nowhere to be found and no way to contact him.

The doctor had already gone home, and the nurses had

to do what they could on their own there in the emergency room. I stood, wringing my hands and whispering prayers.

I watched, so torn! Larry was waiting in the waiting room not knowing what was happening or what to do. I needed Pete but he wasn't there—he was off having 'his time'.

Again I was alone. I knew that Jimmy was breathing, but unconscious. He was not coming to and could see he had begun having seizures. This voice came to me, plain and calm, that the nurses would never be able to save him, and neither could I save him, only the Lord could. I knew then that I was no longer alone and I never had been: God was with me: He was there in the hospital room. He was my 'other' that I'd always looked for.

I took off my jacket, moved to the table where my child lay and began rubbing him in alcohol. Rubbing and praying while the nurses worked alongside me.

I thought about how other mothers loved their children as much as I did mine, and sometimes they still lost theirs. I knew that God is no respecter of persons; I may, and likely would, lose Jimmy. Except for his jerking body, he looked pasty and pale, dead already.

I laid my hands on him and prayed that if he was to go on, for him to go; but if God would let him live, please, please do. As I prayed, I felt a surge of power: God's Power, jolt through my body, down my arms and into my hands to Jimmy. Immediately, he straightened and his small body relaxed. He opened his eyes and looked at me. Prayer and God provided the strength that I needed and brought him through.

The crisis passed. God answered my prayer. The nurses and I embraced and hugged, tears brimming all our eyes. Jimmy would live.

As I still gazed into his face in the photo and look in his eyes, I remember the mighty power of God. Jimmy's eyes are to this day a little off balance as a constant reminder to me of how precious life is and how quickly it can be taken away. Jimmy's eyes are just a little crooked after the horror of almost losing him. I'll never forget. . . and I'll always thank Him for saving my son. To this day, I believe God worked through me; used me, to save Jimmy. I felt His Power. There have been times when God has used me to further his healing. The Bible says that his Disciples (all of us how have been called to Him and are willing to do His work) can do great things. I am blessed to have been a vessel to conduct his Power of Healing.

I wipe my eyes and clear away the tears that have puddled there. I lift more hospital mementos from the box. . .

There was one night I remember Dr. Watts being needed at the hospital but had already gone home. Some of the nurses were off their shift and I was working, keeping watch on the patients, mostly alone. We'd all been instructed (by the patient's family) to call Dr. Watts when that patients from a well-to-do family had a really bad spell. He was expected to die, but the family still wanted Dr. Watts to come---even if there was nothing he could do. When I checked the man, I knew he was in a bad way. I called Dr. Watts.

When he answered the phone and realized it was the hospital calling, I could hear the exasperation in his voice. He said, "Fannie, I told you, I can't come. What does the family expect me to do, die for him?" His voice got tender then. He knew I was only doing what I was supposed to and he told me that I was a wonderful nurse, but I couldn't be so tender. Everybody couldn't be saved. Nursing was hard and I was tenderhearted.

I learned a lot from him and my work at the hospital, and not just things related to healing the body with medicines, but far more than that. People's will to live is affected by love, consideration, and encouragement as well as medication.

I put away the hospital papers and am reminded about Pete's father, Pappa Jim.

Eleven

Our Own Home

Pete and I had been married about five years and still lived in the old Lipham house by the late-1950s. Bowdon High School, located just across the road, wanted to purchase the property we lived on and construct a ball field so we had to move and had nowhere to go. Pappa Jim, Pete's daddy, came to our rescue. He gave us a lot from his property across town for us build a Shell House. A company would come in and build a 'shell'—outer walls, roof, doors and windows, and the owners were responsible for finishing it up. Pappa Jim was good to us.

We took the property and were able to purchase the basic shell of the house. When the shell was completed, Pete and I finished it up. He was working then, part-time, and so he had extra time to work and finish up the house.

We moved in and were proud to have a home and land of our own. There was a branch (small stream of water) along the property and I had high dreams for it. I thought I could dam it up and make fish pond and the children would enjoy bringing their friends and fishing there. We'd have extra fish to eat and that would really help out with our groceries and help us save some money. And people could come and fish and we could charge a little money per pound from their catch and that would help out, too. Most of all, I'd like for people to have a place to come to enjoy being with us and have fun.

I'd seen pictures on TV while I worked days at the hospital. I wanted my sons to have 'up to date' beds and not have to sleep together in one bed but we didn't have any money to buy separate beds. Pete got some two-by-fours and we made two sets of bunk beds. I made mattresses from straw and sewed them up. I was proud that my children didn't have to sleep all bunched up together in one bed like I had with my sisters when I was little. I wanted my children to be raised part in city and part in country: to have the best of both worlds. It was important for them to know what was going on and to experience different environments and opportunities so they would be able to make wise choices when they grew up. Everything we needed I asked God for, and He provided.

The good times didn't last.

Pete was a good man, but he also loved to <u>have</u> a good time. After we got the new house, I had the opportunity to start working at school operating the kitchen (got to use those skills I learned from Ms. Lipham again). I worked during the day and was able to be at home at night.

There in our new house, we had a house full of people all the time. But they were his buddies—not my friends. Many of the men didn't, for the most part, respect me and gave me a hard time. Often they said or did things that were 'out of the way' and I felt really uncomfortable in those situations. I didn't tell Pete about it but tried to put up with it and keep myself apart.

I thought of those times. Times trying to keep peace and keep my marriage working. I had to take care of myself back then; earn money, care for my children, and entertain a houseful of people at a minute's notice. It was so hard, but I realize now that being able to adapt then really taught me things so I can be independent today.

I took care of me and my children, and Pete, too, as best I could. I was still close to God and tried hard to remain close and let Him lead me but with each situation that happened, it got harder. I did and said things I shouldn't have; sometimes drifting away from His teaching. Pete and I didn't fuss much but when he started going out with a wilder crowd and bringing them home, it was almost all I could bear. Prayer kept me holding my marriage together and allowed me to preserve my marriage for a while. I could never have made it all if I had tried it on my own.

I had a sour gut feeling that Pete had a friend, a light colored female friend, and when she came into our home, I could tell something was going on between them. He wouldn't talk much to me about her, but when she came in there was a feeling--a heaviness that bear down and I was miserable.

Times were really hard then, emotionally and financially. Pete worked for a local grocery warehouse and bringing in some extra money helped out a lot. Then there came a time when Pete was laid off from work. During President Eisenhower's term the minimum wage was enacted. The act was supposed to assure households a steady, secure income, but his boss couldn't afford to pay his employees the minimum wage and Pete lost his job. Not being able to bring in money to support his family cost him a lot of pride.

Pete knew it would be hard to pay the bills with only my income. He was compassionate and concerned and would take odd jobs to help out. For a while, Pete did all he could: worked short jobs, took whatever he was offered to keep the land. One time he even helped dig a well. As more time passed he grew unhappier, became depressed, and felt a lot of loss. I think he became to feel less of a husband and father. It was really hard for him. There was a lot more stress filling up our house, and I felt that I had even more responsibility weighing on my shoulders.

Our children were growing up. I kept working so they could have things they needed. They worked and helped out around the house so I wouldn't have so much to do at home. They did many things for me; helping with meals and laundry, keeping the house tidy while I was working.

Hard times didn't end, though. My marriage to Pete was not an easy one, especially during the time he was without work.

It's hard to forget the really bad times, I have learned to forgive, but the hurt and betrayal is hard to forget.

I recall a heart-breaking time. One winter night Pete came in and I had the wood heater red hot. My children needed warmth and as long as I could provide a good place to eat and sleep, I would. We had filled the heater with wood at bedtime and it would keep us warm until morning. We went to bed.

Sometime during the night Pete stumbled in, drunk and helpless, and knocked the heater over. In my desperation, hopelessness, and anger at Pete, I let the devil into my thoughts. An awful thought passed through my mind: what if I could just let him lay there while I got my children out and let the house caught fire and he just burned up?

I came to myself! What a thought! Forgive me God. I got Larry and Eddie to help me, and somehow we got Pete safe and the heater up and the scattered embers cooled. Finally we were all able to get back to bed and to sleep.

I recall another time Pete came home drunk. I had put the children to bed and made sure there was plenty of firewood stacked and fresh water in the drinking bucket. Then I lay down myself. I wasn't sleepy and just in the bed waiting and wondering where Pete was and what he might be doing. Through the darkness, I heard the door opening, someone stumbling around, mumbling and muttering and I knew Pete was home.

For a minute, it was quiet and I relaxed. Then a loud scraping noise and more muttering. I decided I needed to get up and find out what Pete was doing. I padded to the kitchen and pulled on the string hanging from the kitchen light and in its sudden glaring brightness, there he was.

"Pete," I called, moving to the kitchen table where he lay sprawled. He barely raised his head. "Pete," I said again, shaking him by the shoulders. He mumbled something about going to bed. He thought he'd gotten to the bedroom, but instead, pulled his way onto the table and collapsed. I thought that the only way I could get him sober enough to help him to the bed was try and get some cool water down him.

I put my hands on my hips and shook my head in aggravation as I headed to the water bucket. When I raised the dipper, I knew. He had managed to mess up the drinking water before finding his "bed". He had urinated in the water bucket! I grabbed the bucket and threw open the back door and slung that bucket as far out into the yard as I could. I was more than aggravated by then; I was mad, exasperated, and frustrated!

"Pete," I shouted as I slammed the door. "Get up! What do you mean?" Tears were running down my cheeks as I pulled him off the table to his feet and wrapped his arm around my shoulders. He balanced there for a moment and together we teetered through the door into the bedroom. I managed to get his shoes off and helped him lay down. I reached and covered him with a quilt and sat on the side of the bed, my head in my hands. I managed to stop the tears. I was filled with anger mixed with desperation and despair, and finally, I felt a kind of pity for him. I wanted to pound him senseless and hug him close at the same time.

I took a deep breath and tried to clear my head and listen to my heart. He was my husband and I loved him. Even with his drinking and not being able to help out with the children as I wanted him to, or bring in very much money, we had taken vows and I wanted to fulfill them as best I could. I lay down and snuggled under the cover next to Pete. I put my arm over his chest and closed my eyes. The morning sun would come and we both would carry on.

There were good times in that house, too. We made do with things we had around the house to have fun. The children took empty tin cans and punched holes through the bottoms and tied strings through them to connect the cans. These were their 'telephones.' They'd spend hours working to build them and stretching the string tight and talking through the cans and string. They'd make tom-walkers. They'd hammer a piece of wood sideways about two-thirds up a long strip of wood to use as a foot rest, and then hammer up a second so they'd have a pair. They they'd hop on and walk around the yard. It was hard to hold on and balance to stay up, but they did it. We'd laugh and clap our hands when they were tom-walking across the yard.

Then they might make a go-cart. They'd find leftover wood and use pine-tree logs cut for wheels. The carts were wobbly and didn't last long, but they had a fun time riding down hills and see how fast they could go.

Love Lifted Me

I rise and breathe deeply. Those days were so good, even though there were a few trying times. There were so many good things happening then: our own home, my children growing up and finding their musical talents. They could play instruments, a trait inherited from Pete's family.

My children are so blessed to have such strengths and abilities.

Twelve

Dark Winds Begin Blowing

I find some of my girl's baby things. They're faded from so much washing.
   The memories continue . . .

Along these times I noticed there was a man, Clive, and he was often watching me, and was, strangely, around to help me when I was in need. He knew I was having a hard time (but most people in our neighborhood did, too) yet I wondered why he chose to pay <u>me</u> attention. Finally I got up my nerve and asked him about it. He said that it was the most unlikely thing that led him to me; he said he was drawn to me because he noticed how I hung the clothes on the clothes line to dry--like some kind of 'sign' for him that told him that he needed to help me. Odd to me, but he had his own understanding and reasoning, I guessed.
   There was a time I was walking back from the grocery store carrying bags of groceries. Clive had a car and drove by. He wanted to help me get home and offered to give me a ride. I took the welcoming offer.

He visited and came to the house, as many of the people who lived nearby did. I thought of him as a friendly man, and he was a friend to me. I invited him to church – and he went a few times. Little did I know how this man and his 'friendship' would come to haunt me and cause me countless sleepless nights and fill me with unimaginable worry and fear.

Clive didn't ever really press me for anything, simply seemed really sympathetic for my family. We would talk and I learned that he had had a hard time as a boy growing up. His father beat him like a dog. He had a great hatred toward white people. When he saw how I was being treated in mine and Pete's relationship, he felt kindred to me. He felt that I was being mistreated. He opened up to me. I felt sorry for him and wanted to help him.

He seemed harmless enough, but still I was uneasy of him, even a little scared most of the time, knowing the hardness he harbored in his heart. I never really knew what Clive would do. There was an underlying stream of unpredictability racing through him. Even a streak of meanness.

I came to realize that he kept tabs on me; I saw him watching from a distance, even when I worked in the field. A creeping uneasiness and cold fear began growing in the pit of my belly. A forewarning.

I didn't know God's plan; I thought God made all things good, so all I could do was trust Him and keep on keeping on. I kept the uneasy feeling pushed to the back of my mind. Clive was someone I could talk to when I couldn't talk to Pete. He was around when Pete was out doing 'his thing'.

Perhaps I shouldn't have trusted Clive, but I had little else on which to rely.

Thirteen

Trouble, Trouble, Toil and more Trouble

After shuffling through that trunk and putting it away, I move on to a small shoebox. I lift the lid and, sure enough, another piece of paper that throws me back in time...a security deposit.

Our money problems eased a little when Pete found a job in Atlanta, but in the days that passed I learned that Pete still saw his woman-friend. Then things became all mixed up. Her husband got all involved quite by accident.

One night Pete and the woman got to drinking, and they ended up in the late hours of the next morning at her house. That day her husband came home from work during lunch. When he came in he saw a horrible sight: Pete and the woman were lying sprawled on the floor. Dead???

The man ran to a neighbor's for help. When they got back and found the couple, they realized their condition was the result of a drunken, lustful stupor.

When that news came to me, Pete and I had a long talk. Things had finally come to a head. I couldn't handle our living situation any longer. I told him if he loved the woman, take her and go. I would take care of our children. How I would care for seven children, I didn't know, but I knew with

God's help we would manage.

In the end, I realized Pete was my children's father and I wanted to protect them and help them have a family with a father and mother. They deserved a better childhood than I'd had. Pete wanted to stay. He was remorseful and wanted to make things right. We would try to work everything out.

I was with Pete, and would remain faithful.

When Clive realized that Pete wasn't leaving, he left and went to Maryland. I supposed he was angered that Pete and I stayed together.

In spite of all the Pete's drinking and my worries about his unfaithfulness, there were good things that came out of in that house there on 'the hill'. Our children always came first. I knew if they were kept busy and had chaperoned times of fun, they might stay out of trouble. I organized busses to take children to Wedowee, and their parents and I took them to the skating rink and to LaGrange to the swimming pool. We even went all the way to Tennessee to see beautiful waterfalls.

God planned for all this. I knew this was what I needed to do.

One night I was lying down and the window was right next to the bed. I noticed there was a bright light shining in and I wondered about that light. I looked through the window and there was the brightest, whitest, glowing moon. I looked closer and there was a perfect cross in it. God was sending me a sign.

I've never seen anything like that to this day. It came as a comfort and every time I think of that night, the moonlight, and that cross, I feel a special peacefulness.

God was telling me that He was with me. He knows our futures and He is concerned for us. Yet hard times came once more.

Pete's Atlanta job played out and I came to be the lone breadwinner again. I thought Pete could help by looking after the children at home for me while I worked, but he wouldn't do that. Pete was a good man but with no money and lots of time on his hands, good men can do bad things.

Pete and I stayed together and tried to have a happy family. I tried to keep God strong, but there has to be both man and wife working for the same thing and holding God first for a family to grow and be happy.

Days passed and times were hard, if not harder than ever before. I couldn't keep up all the house payments and we finally had to leave. We lost the house.

I didn't think I could bear to have Pete and his drinking, his buddies, his odd and unpredictable behavior, in our next home. I told him he couldn't go with us.

I prayed. I prayed that God would protect Pete and keep him safe. I prayed that my children would prosper and not get in trouble. I prayed that I could be the strong mother that they needed.

God touched my heart and I knew that my prayers were asking God for the easy way out. I knew I had to try to keep my family together, complete with Pete, one more time.

We moved into the projects.

> *For in that he himself hath suffered being tempted, he*
> *is able to succor them that are tempted.*
> Hebrews 2:18

The move didn't help Pete's behavior. After a while I knew then that I had given my all; I had done all God wanted and expected me to do. This was the end. . . Pete had to go—

for good. I had followed God's will and tried one last time. Pete didn't change. I couldn't let him continue to be the unhealthy—and unholy—father figure for our children.

Pete had to move on, and he had to find his way without me. He got his meager belongings and what he had; he tied up in a small cloth bag. It was so sad to see the man I loved and the father of my children leaving our home carrying only a tiny parcel. All his worldly goods—held in one bag. I felt such loss and sadness for him, but knew God's hand was in this move.

I didn't have anything to do with him after that day.

I was alone. My children were almost grown. I was used to working and caring for my house; washing clothes and cooking meals. It was not totally an unhappy time. I felt a great burden lift with Pete gone: no worries about his drinking, his stumbling home, and worry about getting a call that something had happened to him. My children and I worked together and they helped as they could. With the skills I'd learned working with organized, resourceful women when I was young, we managed better than some.

I can honestly say that I loved Pete's family. And they always made me a part of theirs. For that I received another blessing.

Love Lifted Me

Ray, Pete's nephew. A special young man.

Pete's Brother's family. (the girl in blue came and helped out in Dayton)

Fourteen

Don't Be Where You Ought Not To Be

I noticed that after my separation from Pete my former 'friend', Clive, was back in town. Somehow news had traveled fast, and he had learned that Pete had moved out for good. Clive was unexplainably popping up close by me more and more often. He seemed to be around an awfully lot. I tried to be nice but keep my distance.

He really began to put on the pressure to be around me. He'd come by and offer to go to church with me. He'd park his car in front of my house and tell me not to ride with anybody else; he'd take me where I wanted to go. If I drove his car, he checked the mileage to check if I'd been where I said I had. He really tried to control my life.

At last he told me he wanted to marry me. He'd never find another woman like me. We'd take the girls and leave my sons behind, he said. He thought my young men were old enough to take care of themselves; if not, they could get help somewhere.

I couldn't believe this—absolutely not! There was no way I would ever leave any of my children. My childhood was more than enough to prove how much children needed a loving and stable home—single parent or not.

I talked to Clive, explained how I felt about my children, and I tried to help him get closer to God. I tried to be nice to this man; God told me to be kind to him.

He read my kindness the wrong way. Clive put even more pressure on me; hard pressure. I knew that a match with him would lead to no good. But I couldn't fight him and get away. I was frightened of him and grew even more wary of him. I knew I must turn away from him and tried to explain that I would have no life without my family, that God wanted me to be a mother, provider, and protector of my children.

I told him that if I didn't do what God said for me to do, I would be better off dead. And I believed that.

I still didn't see Pete, but heard about how he was doing. On weekends lots of neighbors and friends went to the "Sugar Shack" and had 'good times'. They invited me to go, but I never felt that my life should be going in that direction. I'd seen too many sad occasions arise from being in places like that. Mr. Lipham's words echoed in my heart—words about not getting out doing what other people did and to keep my self-respect. I knew people did go and have their good times, and I knew Pete went.

There was another reason I couldn't go. I'd had a dream where I'd shot someone. It was so real. I didn't know who the man was; Pete, I thought, so I wouldn't go. I feared my dream would come true.

Later I heard about what happened at the Sugar Shack.

Pete and his brother, Jerry and his wife, were at the party. Supposedly, rumor was, Jerry's wife and Clive's brother-in-law had been having an affair. Pete and Jerry had found out about it. They went to the party knowing all involved would probably be there and were looking to clear things up. When they got there they learned Clive's brother-in-law had a gun, but Jerry had come prepared; he had one too.

The story goes that the woman's husband thought Jerry was going to confront him and force the truth from him. He believed it would more than likely get ugly. The man was scared and thought if he didn't shoot Jerry first, Jerry would end up shooting him. The man had Clive with him for extra morale and somehow Clive got the gun and shot Jerry without warning—and killed him. Then, afraid that Pete would try to retaliate, he shot Pete. People scattered.

I was home that night and it was late. There was a knock on the door and I knew in my heart that something was bad wrong. Just by the knock. It was about midnight—I knew the devil is most busy after midnight and felt that evil was about. I went to the door and there was Clive, still holding the gun. The first thing he said, in a flat and sure voice was, "I just shot and killed Jerry and tried to kill Pete. You said you'd be better off dead than not do what God said for you to do. I come to see if you meant it."

There was meanness in his dark, menacing eyes. He just stared at me, his black eyes boring into mine. I remembered my words I'd said to him about doing God's will and knew he meant to kill me.

The Holy Spirit told me to be kind to him. I spoke through the Spirit and told him that he must do what his conscience said for him to do. I stood there facing him and didn't try to run or to scream for help. The Holy Spirit kept me calm. I know I was held in the hand of God for those few minutes.

Clive simply turned around and walked to his car.

The next day I learned that he had run off to his daddy's and the sheriff came and picked him up there later that night.

I heard that Pete was in the hospital. He was alive. I hadn't been with him since our separation and didn't feel that

I should go then. I didn't go.

Clive was jailed. While he was locked up he sent for me to come to see him. The law thought I shouldn't go, told me to stay away for my own protection. I never wanted to go but was afraid not to. I was afraid of him—even the police was afraid of him. I went later, after things calmed down some but that was the extent of my visiting the jail.

A year passed. Talk of the shooting faded and I was able to get back into my routine. But there was always a niggling at the back of my mind concerning Clive. I didn't trust him and had worrisome thoughts about what he might still be able to do, even while he was in jail. He had friends and family and he was very persuasive about getting his way. I heard rumors that there was a trustee at the jail who fed him information about me: where I went, what I did. Clive's fingers reached out from those bars on the jail window into the projects; touching lives and making me uneasy.

It came time for the trial. The night before it began a man came to my house and knocked on the door. I knew him, it was the husband of Pete's former light-skinned female 'friend'. I wouldn't open the door. In times past, when someone came like that at night and they were let in, they brought nothing but bad news. I felt that he carried bad news, and I wouldn't let him in because I didn't want to hear anything to do with unpleasantness.

The next morning, on the day that Clive was going to trial, I noticed all around in the projects where I lived people were getting together. They gathered in bunches and talked in whispers.

Going to the trial together, I thought. I did think it was odd that all this gathering together and whispering was going on this day--since a year had passed and things had settled down, so why all the concern now?

I knew *I* wasn't going to the trial—didn't feel that I could be there in the same room with Clive. I left for work and as moved closer to the groups when I walked by my neighbors, I noticed many had tears in their eyes. I thought to myself, "Why tears? Why should they be crying about Clive's trial?"

I went to school to work, as usual, but I didn't know how to feel. I was in a confused state. Things in the neighborhood that were going on were really odd. It made me think of all that happened: Jerry dead, Pete shot, Clive threatening me, and people in my community acting more than strange that morning.

When I got to school and walked into the lunchroom kitchen, everything was the same with me as always. I began working, preparing for the day. I was the head of the lunchroom at that time, and the principal came to me and he wore a concerned look on his face. He explained that I didn't have to come in and work, that I could leave and they could get someone to work in my place. He urged me to go back home for the day due to all that had happened. I assured him I could was fine; I could work. He nodded his head and returned to his office.

I was puzzled. I realized that more was going on than simply Clive's trial and I was totally in the dark. "What in the world?" I thought.

Then someone came to me and asked if I'd not heard about Barbara Jo burning up? Barbara Jo—Pete's long-time woman friend. Fear overwhelmed me. The first thought was Clive: had he been able to contact someone and reach his evil out from his jail cell and touch Barbara Jo to cause the fire as a deadly threat to anyone who might testify against him? A warning to me?

Or maybe it was simply a coincidence. Maybe Barbara Joe fell asleep with a lit cigarette and the whole thing was simply an accident.

I was devastated. The crying came; I broke down. I knew

I couldn't go home, my children were there at school and I needed to be near them.

Another thought hit me--like a huge bucket of cold water had been poured over me. I realized why that man came to the house the night before. He knew about the fire and had come to tell me. I'd had hard feelings about the relationship between Barbara Jo and Pete. I blamed her for a lot of our worries. There was a black spot in my heart because of her, but with the horror of her death, I knew I had to go to the Lord and get my life clean; seek forgiveness. I prayed for her, for me to find forgiveness, and for Pete. Slowly the hurt and anger was lifted. The Lord gave me peace once again.

I went to the principal's office to let him know that I'd had no idea of what had happened to Barbara Jo when he talked with me that morning. Now I needed his understanding and support. He led me to the break room and left me for a time of peace so that I could pull myself together.

I moved to the window. I stood looking out that window and I prayed. I saw an image: the bluest, clearest sky, then crystal clear sparkling water. I saw people coming onto shore walking on the water. The Spirit came and began to surround me. A beautiful comfort began to envelope me and a voice spoke within me---'wipe away your tears'.

My tears were gone. To this day, my tears are gone. For some reason, I cannot cry; cannot shed any tears. This is a mystery, but at that day, the Spirit truly took away my tears.

It was a beautiful vision that led me to the understanding that I needed to leave Bowdon. Yet, how could I go when I had no money!

I thought of Mrs. Lipham, and how she always said to have faith, how faith can move mountains, and to simply have the faith as a tiny mustard seed and I could succeed. I remembered how she told me to have faith in You, Almighty God. All my fears drained. All I must do is trust in Him. His Word from St. Matthew came to mind:

> *If thou wilt be perfect, go and sell that thou hast and give to the poor, and thou shalt have treasure in heaven; and come and follow me. Matthew 19:21*

There, standing by that window, looking at the image of the clear sky and blue water, a line of the Spirit's circle formed, moved and connected, surrounded and embraced me with peace and love. I knew God had been training me, leading me to the time and place where I could go and grow. I realized I'd closed a gap that held me in Bowdon.

It was time to move.

The things on which Mrs. Lipham had taught me to rely had come to fruition. I had listened to her and knew what should be done, but never had to actually act on her words. The Spirit's circle's ends had joined around me and the circle was complete; my feelings were healed. Back in that time when I was working for her, Mrs. Lipham had no idea how much I would come to depend on her guidance and words of faith.

The presence of God was real as I stood and gazed out into that beautiful sky. I went back and told principal that I was fine; I could finish the day.

Fannie Billingsley Cooley Sullivan

...The kingdom of Heaven is like to a grain of mustard seed, which a man took, and sowed in his field: Which indeed is the least of all seeds; but when it is grown, it is the greatest among herbs, and becometh a tree, so that the birds of the air come and lodge it the branches thereof. Matthew 13: 31-32

Fifteen

A Bloody Night

They all hold swords, being expert in war; every man hath his sword upon his thigh because of fear in the night.
Song of Solomon 3:8

Clive's trial was held the next day, and he received only a year's conviction. So little and so sad for murder and attempted murder. And to make matters worse, since he'd already served a year, they let him out.

The stalking began again.

I couldn't handle that. Clive wanted to be with me. I told him that was impossible. He'd killed Jerry and shot my children's daddy.

Nevertheless, he still had friends about and even people in the projects reported to him; my neighbors. He had them watching me; <u>he</u> watched me.

One night he stopped me as I returned home. I saw the devil in his eyes. His voice was filled with venom as he hissed and spat that he was going to kill me. I didn't doubt him one bit. He'd killed before and was threatening me a second time. I didn't know what to do. With all my heart I believed that he would find a way to end my life unless I did as he wanted me to.

I was terrified. Each step I took, I moved in fear. I felt that I was in a closed, dark box and couldn't find a way out, and no one could get in to help me. I had to do something to persuade Clive to move on. If he didn't, I knew there would be an explosion. He was pushing me, backing me into a corner and I knew I'd have to fight my way out. But I never thought that I could hurt anyone. I wasn't a fighter; I never liked confrontations and had always tried to stay out of trouble.

Nor could I think of anyone to stand up for me and stop him. Lots of people were afraid of him, and most people who knew him gave him a wide space.

I knew that Clive had often threated, and meant the threat, that if anyone ever tried to hurt him they'd better kill him when they came on or he'd turn around and finish them off. He was the type of man who backed up his words.

Every sound I heard was him attacking me. I watched every move around me. My life was in torment. I was a nervous wreck.

My only answer was from the Holy Spirit. That voice told me to talk to Rev. Wilder the next time I went in clean his house. My part-time work, cleaning and working after school lunchroom hours, added much to my income.

Rev. Wilder, the pastor of the white folks' Methodist Church in Bowdon, was a great shepherd for the Methodist church flock. He was a strong man and helped anyone in times of need. He listened to all the people's problems and prayed and let the Lord lead him.

The next day when I went in to work for the Reverend, I broke down and told him about Clive's death threat. I had to get it off my chest. I was terrified and didn't know who I could go to for help. I had to have some peace. Many people couldn't believe or understand how I felt and couldn't offer advice. Clive was a powerful man. I didn't know if it came down to him or me if I could stand up to him or not. I truly felt that I could never hurt anyone---not even him.

Rev. Wilder had realized something was wrong as soon as I got there. I had to let the story go. I opened up and all my fears, my frustrations, and desperation poured out.

Rev. Wilder asked me all kinds of questions, especially what Clive had done out of the way, what kinds of things he'd said, how he acted toward me, and how controlling he was. After hearing the whole story, he believed then, like I did, that Clive was intent on killing me if I didn't cooperate with his wishes.

Rev. Wilder explained that Clive was like a snake. He told me that I must take care of myself. He said what I already knew: if Clive followed through on his threat, my children would be homeless, without a mother. I knew there was nothing I could say or do to stop Clive. If he was a snake, I was his prey.

Rev. Wilder feared for me. He knew Clive and he knew me. He, too, believed that Clive would kill me if he couldn't have his way.

Rev. Wilder gave me a gun. I didn't want to take it. I couldn't see the need of me having it--I knew I could never shoot it. Even the thought of shooting someone in the leg just to stop him made my stomach turn. Rev. Wilder told me that he believed if Clive knew I had a gun he would stop and think—I had gotten myself a weapon and *I* could hurt *him*. I felt better that Clive might leave me alone.

Rev. Wilder explained that if Clive did come for me, I had to defend myself or I'd be dead. I knew if Clive ever came by and wanted in, I would never open the door. If he had the nerve to break in my house he'd be there for only one purpose—to fulfill his deathly threat. Still, I couldn't fathom me actually pulling the trigger.

Rev. Wilder accompanied me home and as he carried the gun into my house, he held it in his hand for everyone around to see, wanting all the neighbors to see it and know I had protection. Even then, I thought it was for show; to make me safer. Rev. Wilder thought the gun was a good warning, and, knowing I had it, Clive would surely leave me alone.

I put the gun on the table in the living room in plain sight. In my heart I thought that just having the weapon would make me safer; anyone coming into my house with thoughts of harming me would see it and leave, and I'd never have to shoot it. Surely the sight of a gun would scare Clive away.

I left the gun out. I reasoned that when Clive's in the projects he'll hear about it. I made sure people could see it in passing. I thought if I let them see the gun, they'll tell him and then he'd know I meant my words. I needed something I could see and touch; a formidable protection like the gun.

I got ready for bed. All my children were there except Larry and Willa. Larry was old enough to be out by then and Willa was spending the night with her godmother. I put the others to bed. Then I lay down and began reading my Bible. I prayed. I was asking God to help me, sustain me. There were simply too many emotions filling me to be able to relax.

It seemed like there was a storm brewing outside, and it threw dark menacing shadows across my room. When I looked up from my bed, there appeared a picture on the wall---like picture printed of Jesus. Suddenly, there were words I could hear; plain words just like people speaking, forming in my room. I knew He was telling me what to do, 'just listen to Jesus'. I understood.

Through my prayers and hearing the comforting words, my nerves calmed. Whispering, encouraging, strengthening words came and continued speaking to me.

There was a streetlight shining into my room so I could see, almost bright as day. The words came to me: "Take the gun and hide."

The air felt electrified. Something was about to happen; coming to a head. I was wide awake and wary, yet conflicted with other feelings: calm yet tense and wary.

I knew Clive was about—I could feel him. I slipped to the living room and picked up the gun. I waited quietly, gripping the gun in my lap, hoping that nothing would happen and I could return to bed. Suddenly there was a man standing outside the door, silent and bold, on the stoop. He had slithered up quietly, like a rattlesnake getting ready to strike. He didn't knock. I stared through the glass in the door and I could see the outline of his face. He turned his head and looked one way down the street, then the other, coiling around to see if anyone was watching. We were alone. I felt like I was in a horror movie, but this was real.

I watched. A fleeting thought passed through my mind: there was supposed to be a police detective outside on duty; protecting my house, but he was not there. Why wasn't he there, helping me? Where was he?

My breath stopped as the man outside shattered the small window in the door. To me it sounded loud enough for the whole neighborhood to hear. My eyes followed his hand as it stealthily glided in through the broken glass and his probing fingers moved to unlock the door. Quietly and slowly the door swung open—seemingly almost in slow motion. He was standing, silhouetted in my doorway. I felt the devil himself was about to step into my home.

I didn't realize I was holding my breath. My heart was beating so hard it seemed that it would burst from my chest. I heard a roaring in my ears.

Shoot him in the leg, my mind screamed, before he gets to you. I was gripping the gun so tightly my fingers ached. I could hardly breathe, only quick gasps came. It was like I was in another place and this wasn't really happening; almost like

I was on the other side of the room and was watching as this nightmare unraveled.

The idea of wounding him was knocked away when I heard his hissing voice: "You'd better kill me when you have the chance or I'll turn and get you for good."

A voice shouted in my head, "Raise gun and stop him! Now! Just shoot!"

I closed my eyes and prayed and time stopped.

To this day, don't remember pulling the trigger. I just shot. It's hard to believe it really happened.

Before the thunderous noise of the gun stopped echoing in my ears, I threw it down. I opened my eyes and I couldn't believe what I was seeing. He was coming at me! I turned and began running, down the hall, through my room, to my daughter's room, and yanked open her bedroom door.

I could hear the echo of his footsteps following, coming down the hall after me. I was never so scared in my life. My hands trembled. My knees were like rubber and my breath came in shallow gulps. Somehow I raced across the room and jerked open a window and hollered to my neighbor, "Come get my children; call the police!"

I still couldn't believe he might be dead; I thought he was only wounded and would still get me. At any second it seemed I would feel his hand grabbing me, pulling me back, or feel a hard jolt of searing pain as I was hit by bullet.

The police came. I begged and cried as I pleaded for them to take me to jail—I thought Clive was still alive and I would be protected, safe from him there.

All this while my children were in the house. They were awakened when they heard the noise, the gun, my screams, not knowing what could have happened to cause all the commotion. They felt the terror as well.

Later as Jimmy recalled the events, he said as he came running through the house to find me, he thought he saw Clive's heart hanging from his chest as he passed the body slumped in the hallway. My heart ached for my son: What an awful image to carry for the rest of his life.

I knew I'd have to stay at the jail because of the shooting. Police asked me if I'd like to make a phone call and I knew I had to call Rev. Wilder. When I reached him and he spoke to me on the phone, he said he had been in his pulpit praying and meditating when he heard a voice and experienced a flash of lightning. He realized he must leave the church *right then*, knew that something had happened to Fannie and he needed to get home to the phone. When the phone rang, he said, he knew it was me. He came to the jail immediately.

The police told me that I'd not have to stay in jail, but I needed to stay with someone I knew—I couldn't go back to my home, the crime scene. I went to Mozell's, Larry's aunt on his father's side. My kind neighbors, my true friends, had taken in the children while I was being processed at jail.

When I finally got to Mozell's, she went and gathered the children and brought them to me. We stayed there days and days. We couldn't go back to our apartment. I couldn't imagine ever going back into that place. Too, Clive had friends and family all in the projects. I was still afraid that they would take revenge on either me or my children.

So much happened in such a short time. Barbara Jo's death, Clive's trial, and the shooting. My plans for leaving Bowdon were put on hold. I had to stay and take responsibility for what had happened.

Sixteen

Moving On

...a faded newspaper clipping...Shootings always make the news...

Then came MY trial. When we got to the courtroom, I saw that Clive's daddy came along with most of his family. I was asked so many questions and had to relate the story once more, just as it happened.

I said I was sorry, heartbroken, that I hadn't wanted to do the deed that I had done. During the trial I wanted to do all I could to ease everyone's pain and release my children from their fears. It was a scary, uncertain time.

Clive's family seemed to understand and no warrant was taken out for me. The shooting was ruled in self-defense. Oh, how I thanked God!

Still, I couldn't sleep; couldn't go back to my home. I finally found another house but was still afraid. I didn't know what Clive's friends would do—never mind the law's results. The police understood and gave permission to have someone stay near my family for protection until I decided what to do.

All Clive's kinfolks and friends were around close by. In spite of their proclamation that they understood my actions, I felt that they wanted retribution. Even in Clive's death, I still lived in fear.

My sister, Virgello, wanted me to come to Dayton to be with her family there. I would be away from any possible danger I faced in Bowdon, and we would be safe. But, again, how to go so far with seven children and no money?

After the shooting, folks who knew me, those I'd worked with, treated me the same as they always had. I suppose they understood how I felt and knew how desperate I was at that time, and how I did the only thing I could to survive.

I went to Mrs. Smith, a woman I worked for part time, and discussed my problem. I knew the move was the best thing, but how was I to move?

She said, "Fannie, I don't know what is about you, but I think you should go and see if you like it; go and see, leave the children here for a few days and check it out. Then you can come back and get the children if you think y'all can make it there. I believe you can make it anywhere you go."

She gave me confidence. I knew God would help, too. Up until then, I don't think I truly had confidence to make such a move. I was so broken down after Clive's stalking and oppression and the stigma of being a murderer (even in self-defense). I had always thought I was strong and was able to help myself but had never faced such a huge decision as this.

For God hath not given us the spirit of fear; but of power, and of love and of a sound mind.
2 Timothy 1:7

When I moved, my children moved with me. Somehow we got our bags packed, but I didn't know anything about the process of moving. So many things were involved that I'd never dealt with: finding a new job, getting the children enrolled in school, finding my way around in Dayton. I would be the country girl in a big city; a mighty challenge.

I relied on the Minnifields---again. They helped us move in two cars, one that carried our belongings, and one with me and the children. We carried only a TV, a few household belongings, and our clothes.

I left Bowdon on faith. I'd asked God before we left to provide work for me right off. I needed it the next day when we got to Dayton, I added, and asked Him to please have it there for me. I was counting on finding a job fast so I could get a place of my own.

I didn't know what I would be facing, what conditions were there. All I knew was that my life was changing and I had to hold onto God and trust in Him to lead me. I had to keep my heart open and be aware of the opportunities He would provide.

Seventeen

Dayton or Bust!

We traveled long, crooked roads. It seemed that we rode and rode, but we finally got to Verjello's boarding house. We arrived on Labor Day weekend. When we got there, my seven children and I had one big room for all of us to stay in. We had three fold-away beds to sleep on. There was no more room; my sister couldn't give up boarders in other rooms for us because she depended on that money coming in for her needs. My brother, Booker T. was there as a border and there was also another man renting there.

Oh, on that hot Saturday, we had nothing, really. I had six dollars left after paying the gas money for the trip. No food, no real expense money, no job. – Just each other.

To help us out, Virginia took Larry to live with her and her son who was about Larry's age. That gave us a little more space, and Larry was fine with the move since he had someone his age to help him get familiar with our new city.

Before we left home, some people said I'd have to give up my country ways when got to the bright city lights. In turn, I said if my way didn't go the city folk's way, they'd just have to try my way. I didn't realize just how those words would ring true. I'd have to live them--not just speak them.

I found out soon that people in that part of Dayton didn't go out until near midnight. There was a lot of drinking and partying---made me think of those folks back home and the Sugar Shack. That night I went to the Labor Day party with them, but I asked for orange juice to drink instead of something stronger. They told me that if I didn't follow along with their ways they wouldn't let me go with them anymore. They thought it was funny that I didn't 'join in'. The next night they went out again—without me---my choice.

On Monday morning I told Virgello that I needed a job. I only had a dollar left for each child, and I had to have some money coming in.

I quickly learned that most people could 'buy' the better jobs there in Dayton. However, I learned that I must live in the city for so long a period before could get a higher paying job---just a city rule. If I had been in the city for any length of time, I would have recommendations and could 'buy' work in factories or business. Since I had only arrived and didn't have any local references, I had to use those I had from home. I helped my sister in the boarding house for three days while I looked for work. After three days, I realized I qualified for one job in Dayton that I had been offered: a maid job for Jewish people. I ended up getting domestic work, less pay, but work.

My background was paying off! I was a good housekeeper and knew how to do so many things in a home. I would make $40.00 a week and get an additional fifty cents a day for riding the bus to and from work. I was confident in my ability to do a good job but didn't know much about people of the Jewish faith. But I was ready to learn about that, too.

I took the job.

I settled in and worked. When it came time to enroll the

children in the 1962-63 school year, I was surprised to find that I had to purchase their books, and they would have to have the books before they could be enrolled. I called back 'home' and asked my friend, William "Bill" Harvell, (The Goatman) if I came back to Bowdon and brought my payroll check, would he cash it so I could buy books for the children. He said he would--and he did. With that money, I got back to Dayton and got the children in school.

To this day I am thankful for Mr. Harvell. He was a good man who helped me, as well as a lot of folks, out in many hard times. He cashed checks for me when no one else would, and I had borrowed money from him before when I needed it, and he trusted me to repay him.
I always did and he helped me this time when I needed help.

I was eager to get my children in our own house and on a stable schedule as soon as possible. I was fortunate that we only had to stay in the boarding house with my sister about three months. While we were staying with her, Rose who had been living in California, visited us. She and Daddy were coming through Dayton on their way to get Daddy back home to Gadsden. It was in that short stay that he talked to me about Mother. He never had before. He said, as I remembered he had when I was so small, that mother was the only true love he'd ever had. She was a good woman, he told me, and he'd never found another like her.

He encouraged me to get my children out of that boarding house into a place where they could grow and I could continue working. He wanted, as well as I did, for me to keep working and stay off welfare. I wanted to set a good example.

. . . a good woman. He'd never find another like her. Those were the same words Clive had said to me all that time ago—that he'd never find another woman like me.

Rose and Daddy left, on to Alabama. That was the last time I saw or spoke to my Daddy. I appreciate that he lived the life before me that he did: I never saw him drunk or heard him talk bad about anybody. He died and I never even made it to his funeral...

I found a house, but since Pete and I were still legally married and he would have to sign papers along with me (an impossible thing), I was denied any money to buy it. As bad as it hurt, I knew I must divorce Pete in order to become independent. I got the divorce and was able to buy a house for my children and me.

All this time I had the need to find a church. My siblings weren't involved in a church at that time, so they had no recommendations for me. I prayed that God would lead me to my perfect church family.

After I became financially able to move my family into a home of our own, I finally got involved in a nearby church----just the place where God meant for me to be. I was excited and happy. At last I was getting back into a closer relationship with God and was with people of his flock. I met lots of people, all kinds, and I fit right in. (being poor helped me fit in). The church family, my children, and I joined together and sang. I loved the singing and worship.

The church family realized that everybody needs somebody to lean on and they let me lean on them. When people who never had anyone to lean on find Jesus, and they can lean on Him, then they can get up. With my church family and Jesus, how could I fail?

I learned that a new building was being built and the church was funding it. I was put to work almost immediately and was head of the committee to help raise money. We set a goal of $1,000 to be raised. If everyone could put in $100, we would make our goal. To help us reach our goal I encouraged people to put in a little at a time. I knew that most people, like me, couldn't possibly contribute their whole part at once. God worked and we met our goal! I loved being a part of the success of an active and worthy project.

There's a great lesson in our attempt to raise money. We must remember to not get overwhelmed when the task looks too big, just do at little at a time, work in God's timeline, and great things will happen.

On one occasion our church planned to travel, caravan-style, to a revival in a sister church. The trip would take several hours and Tim was going along. After the hearty lunch at the church, cars lined up and we began to load. I would be riding in one of the front cars and Tim would be in another car, riding with some of his friends. He was only about six or seven, but already becoming independent and able to make (what I thought) good choices. I prided myself on teaching my children to be able to reach out and be able to get along without my constant hovering.

I went to his car and made sure he was loaded. "Now Tim," I said, "You stay in this car and don't get out for anything. I'll be just ahead and will check on you when we stop on down the road."

"Yes, Mama," he replied, his little eyes trusting and sparkling with excitement.

I walked to my car and as the pastor looked back at the line of cars to be sure everyone was ready to go, he stuck his arm out the window, started the ignition, and waved the line on as we pulled into the road. We looked like a modern-day wagon train getting underway.

We chatted and laughed as the miles swished under the wheels; discussed what we thought about the revival and soon it was time to stop for gas. The line pulled in to the service station and prepared to fill up.

I went to check on Tim.

He wasn't in the car.

"Where is Tim?" I almost shouted at the passengers in the car.

One little boy, his eyes huge, fearfully admitted, "Well, Miss Fannie, somebody came and got in with an extra fried chicken leg and Tim wanted one. He hopped out and ran back to the dining hall to get him one. He tried to hurry, but the cars left before he got back."

I stood. Well fine and dandy, I thought. I'd told that little imp to stay put. I understood, though, how those good chicken legs could sidetrack a young child.

I got to a phone and called the church. Sure enough, Tim was still there. I asked to speak to him.

"Tim, I'm so glad you stayed there at church. That was a good thing to do. Now, do you think you can ride the Greyhound if I can get you taken to the station? Will you be afraid? I can meet you when the bus gets to Columbus."

"No, Mama, I won't be afraid. I can ride the bus," he answered. "I want to be with you at the revival."

"Let me speak to the adult there," I said. She agreed to take Tim to the station and get him a ticket. He was 'tagged' and put on the bus.

When I met him the next morning about two a.m., the driver laughed. "He's been right here with me at the front of the bus," he said. "He has behaved so well, just like a little man. He sure has been trained the right way," he remarked.

Tim jumped, tired and sleepy, down into my arms. I gave him a hug and we went back to our friend's to get some sleep. I smiled. Bet Tim would never get left anywhere again!

I worked three years for the Jewish couple. I was polite and I tried really hard to do a good job. I remembered the things from Miss Minnifield and Mrs. Lipham: how to communicate and how to make the house look pretty and neat. Miss Mary, my teacher, taught me to remember things—not just information found in books, but 'learning' things, to put them in my head and when I needed them, I could pull them back out. She was right.

My employer's friends noticed my work and manners and asked where I came from. (They were surprised I came from the south. They had their own ideas about people from the south and I---and many others---just didn't fit their stereotypical ideas!) My employer's visitors told my employers that they liked what they saw in me and asked if I might know anyone who might come to work for them. I told them I knew some people but they may not be like me, everyone had their own ways.

During my time working there the Jewish people warned me not to talk to their children about Jesus. I explained about Him to their little girl only after she asked me about 'my Jesus'. I wasn't preaching, just answering her questions.

My employer's husband was a lawyer and she was a schoolteacher. They were always nice to me. Sometimes they would leave and go to some program or function and let me babysit. Their daughter asked all kinds of questions. She wanted to know why black people were marching in streets: I tried to explain about civil and equal rights. Again she wanted to know about this man Jesus. And I told her. She thought about that a minute, then said that when she grew up, she would go to school and help her people—the Jews.

She did grow up and go back to her country, Israel.

An odd thing I noticed was when I was asked to mop the floors was that there wasn't anything to use other than a bucket and a brush. I didn't object to that chore and asked where I could find the mop. My employer looked confused. I learned that the help was expected to get on their knees and scrub the floor with stiff hand brushes. I talked to her and explained that in the south we had mops. She got me a mop, and I never had to get down on my knees.

That answered another question I'd wondered about. When I rode the bus I noticed women riding with me had rusty-looking, rough knees. I just didn't know why they looked that way. Learning about their 'northern' mopping technique gave me the answer.

I noticed, too, the day workers were always dressed up on the bus and wondered how they could be maids and not dress in a maid's outfit like me. Later I realized they changed clothes when they got to work, and again before leaving to come home. I had always put mine on before I left home and kept it on 'til I got back. I guess they thought I was the odd one!

I learned the city was certainly not like the country. As long as I lived in the country---the south, I never had to go to in the back door of my employers' houses. I learned that in the city, people, day-working people, could go in front door but the folks would talk about them and stab them in the back.

Every day when I rode the bus to work there was a very special bus driver. He was a great help to me—raising my spirits and eventually helping raise my children, especially my sons.

I say 'sons' because all too many times young black men from that time heard jeers,
"Hey, Boy!"
I never called my sons 'boys', that was a term that blacks hated; a put-down. We also called all our elders Auntie and Uncle.
Just terms of respect.

This bus driver was good looking, slightly wavy black hair

and light skinned--almost like a Mexican. The saying was then that that if you had light skin you are white and if your skin is black, you're a nigger. That ain't so. People are who they are regardless of their skin color or hair style.

All the women whispered and talked about how nice that driver looked. Back then the blacks had to sit in the back of the bus. One day he invited me to sit in the front! He had heard me say that I was new in Dayton. He wanted to help me. And he did. He'd buy me candy or chewing gum. He'd listen and I told him my story. I also invited him to the church I'd started attending.

I found out that he was also a detective----in a surprising way. To make sure I hadn't been lying about what I'd told him, he came to my church. Thank goodness I didn't skip services that day! He knew I told the truth so he felt safe offering me help.

And he did help me in many ways. When the bus drivers met together each morning to start their day he told them about me, and they all let me sit in the front.

Nobody believed I had come from the south. Most folks they'd met from the south brought their hate with them. I had had a blessed growing-up. Whites were good to me. I didn't feel any animosity toward them and didn't bring any hate with me. People noticed. The love I held for everyone shined through and that spirit was recognized by the people who wanted to bring a peaceful air to the land. I was treated so wonderful. I remembered the scriptures that God promised He'd bless me in the country and bless me in the city.

Fannie Billingsley Cooley Sullivan

And I will make them and the places round about my hill a blessing; and I will cause the shower to come down in his season; there shall be showers of blessings.
Ezekiel 34:26

Eighteen

Bearing All Burdens

Take my yoke upon you, and learn of me; for I am meek and lowly in heart; and ye shall find rest unto your souls.
Matthew 11:29

The third year I worked as a maid my oldest daughter, then sixteen, told me she had been raped while on a date. My youngest daughter's period never came on regular so when I took the oldest to the doctor for an exam concerning the rape, I took the youngest along to try to get her regular and make sure nothing was wrong.

After the girls were examined, the doctor came out to me. "Mrs. Cooley, sit down, I have something to tell you. Your oldest girl is pregnant due to the rape and the youngest is also pregnant and further along than oldest."

"Whooo," I said, "Lord, how much more do you want me to bear?"

Somehow I bore the shock and got back to work and told the Jewish lady about my girls. She advised me to give away the babies because the girls were underage: they were only seventeen and fifteen years old. She didn't think I could take care of all of them on what I made. She insisted the babies would have a good adoptive home and the girls would be able finish school. She was adamant that they get their education.

She made good sense but I could never give away my grandbabies. I knew all too well about what could happen when little children were 'given away'. I knew that we would make it as long as we kept God in our lives and trusted Him to provide.

All I could do was shake my head and say, "No, Mam. I have grandbabies coming, I want to know them. I want to know my grandchildren; where they are and who they are. I want them to grow up and know about their parents; their family. They'd never be given away, no matter how hard times get."

Somehow I kept the girls in school. Larry, who was almost grown by then, also suggested that the girls quit school and take care of their babies. I couldn't let them do that. That's what I'd had to do when I had mine. I wanted them to get their education and learn to take care of themselves and their babies—do better than me.

When the babies came, Wilma Jean's baby came in June, which was a bit early, and Willa's came in July.

Wilma Jean's baby, which was expected to be born after Willa's but came prematurely, weighed only about two and a half pounds and I could hold that little girl in my hand. She stayed in an incubator for three months. She was strong and had stamina; God was so good! Wilma Jean's baby's daddy tried to marry her but she wouldn't marry because of being forced when she got pregnant. I don't know what was in Jean's mind, I suppose the rape was such a traumatic time that she wanted to forget it, (and I knew how hard that was) and she wanted to marry out of love and respect. She chose to raise her child herself. She loved that baby.

Since Willa was so young, I never really considered her marrying her baby's father. I had so much on me and knew having two babies in the house would make our lives more difficult, but I would never fuss about her decision. We talked about her options but it was up to Willa and the baby's daddy. She chose to raise her own baby. Willa was always so smart in school and was determined to graduate and raise her baby.

They made the right decisions. It may have been hard for all of us, but the blessings and happiness those two little baby girls brought into our lives far outweighed the hardships.

The girls never missed any length of school. The babies were born summer babies so the girls went right back to school in the fall. I paid daycare for the babies so the girls could go to school and I could continue working.

We never had to accept Welfare. Both my girls graduated high school.

To get by, I'd cook a big pot of chili on Monday for the children and make a big pan of biscuits. We called biscuits "light bread". We'd eat that and still have enough for leftovers. Then on Wednesday I'd make a big pot of vegetable soup that would carry us two days. The girls and my sons learned early on to do things for themselves. They could clean and do laundry. They even cooked when they wanted to so we got by just fine.

One thing I didn't allow: I refused to buy my children any candy, but they were smart children. They'd find a way to get some sweets. Most of the families in the city bought their bread already baked in loaves. They'd have toasted bread or make sandwiches and homemade biscuits were rare. The neighborhood children loved our homemade bread and it was a treat for them when they visited our house. My children used the other children's craving to their advantage: they'd take my biscuits and sell them to the neighborhood children and then have their candy money!

I'd work during the day and go to school at night at the

local high school--adult studies. We had the same books as day school and had to pay for our night classes. Anyone who attended had to want to go to better themselves and it was hard for many, me included since it wasn't free. At one time, Wilma Jean and I were in the same Political Science class!

All during this time, I worked days at several different jobs and went to school for three years. Mr. Mills, the state representative who taught history during the night classes, offered to help me during my breaks. I was eager to learn—my dream of getting my diploma was finally coming true! I wanted to find out as much and learn as much as I could and graduate. I thought my options were more than a few: I was finally coming to truly believe that I could become whatever I chose to be.

He explained much about history and how our government works. He taught me about filibusters —one party having long speeches against the other. That word was a strange and somewhat funny one to me. He told me all I wanted to know about questions I had. I learned about senators and the basics of how the government works. Finally I finished my core, or basic classes.

Along with my other classes, I took classes toward becoming a nurse. I had loved working in the hospital back home.

I stopped reminiscing and reached to turn on the light. Funny, I thought, how God takes us through so many roads. Sometimes there are roadblocks or the road is washed out or reaches a dead end. But He always has a detour planned for us and as long as we stay on the right road, He brings us to such a better place than where we'd started. I never became a nurse, but His detour brought me to so many good places. The light fell on a piece of paper, one of my school records, which had slipped to the floor. . . the late 60s had arrived!

For many teachers in Dayton, their night jobs were a

second job. My math teacher, Mr. Stringer, was also the principal. He had to do this to increase his small income from his school position. While I was in his class, he encouraged me to lift up my tongue so that I could speak with clearer diction so those listening could better understand what I said. He wasn't trying to put down my speech or dialect but help me learn to communicate plainly—in any situation. It was a good thing; a valuable lesson that I was to use so much as I grew in faith and works. It was important to know how to speak correctly so that when the opportunity arose, I could make a good impression. I never forgot my roots, though. Knowing when and how to communicate is vital in anyone's life.

All the teachers were good. They worked hard and so did we students.

I went to the unemployment office to try to find a summer job just to fill in my income. I completed the paperwork. As they read over my references and previous jobs they noticed that I'd worked in a hospital, for a school system, and for several well-educated people. Because of that, they said there was nothing there for me; said it looked like my qualifications were too high for what jobs they had to offer. I couldn't understand why they would say that.

I didn't get a job.

I found it hard to realize that I wasn't qualified when I had so much experience and could work in so many different areas.

I wanted to be treated equally. It was hard not to feel anger and become negative. Yet again, I had to put aside my bad feelings and rely on what I knew God had in store for me.

I put away my certificate from night school that I had been holding all this time. I was tired. It was time for bed. The boxes filled with my life story could wait until morning.

Nineteen

God Opens Windows When a Door is Shut

I woke eager to continue organizing my mementoes. Up and refreshed, I settled down in my chair and reached to the bottom of a near box and pulled out a newspaper article.

Ah, I thought. This brings back memories.

About the time I had been turned down at the unemployment office, I learned there was a breakfast program being initiated at my children's school. I learned that the program was in place but found it odd that so many students didn't participate.

I was active in my children's education. When there was something needed, I did my best to help get it. I was in their school often, volunteering and visiting. I was involved in P.T.O, I sewed costumes for class plays, worked with fundraisers, and was around the school on a weekly basis. Whatever the children were involved in—so was I.

I soon heard about black teachers having a kind of attitude. They seemed to have gotten so high and mighty and full of themselves because most of their husbands were not as educated as they were. And, they thought their husbands ran around on them and had 'outside' children and some of those children were right there in the same school and would be eligible for breakfast. Those teachers wouldn't treat those children right. They thought negatively about the 'outside' children—those conceived outside their marriage and didn't want them to have advantages over their own children.

Then, there were simply some parents wouldn't let children come for breakfast for whatever reason.

The principal, Mr. Field, came to me and said the breakfast program would have to be shut down if there were not enough children participating. He knew me because I lived nearby, was active in the neighborhood, and was involved in my children's education. The principal explained that he couldn't get children to come eat breakfast and was disappointed in his teachers for not urging the students to participate. He realized that his faculty caused a lot of the problem but was helpless to correct it.

And he knew me. He knew where we lived and that many of those children eligible for breakfast lived near me—in the same neighborhood. Their parents knew me. The school was not even a block from our house. The job was very tempting: no more riding the bus to domestic work. I'd be close to my children and I'd be able to use the lunchroom skills I'd learned in Bowdon.

I considered it. I prayed about it. I knew I would miss the family I'd gotten so close to where I was working, but I let the Lord lead. I took the job.

The disappointment I'd felt at the unemployment office was lifted. I saw how God does open a new, greater window when one is closed.

Kids began piling in for the program. I treated them good. Even though the school was technically segregated, there were a few white teachers and I had only one white child in the program. After about two months, children were coming in and the Federal Breakfast Program was such a success that a local newspaper interviewed me to find out why there had been such a turnaround in participation. I was proud of what was being accomplished at the school. I was thankful that God had provided opportunities for me to be in good places and learn about communication, organization, cooking skills, and leadership skills when I was growing up. The job was a wonderful one. I loved cooking and organizing the aspects of the program. It was good for me as well. I had come to a place where people had gotten to know me and knew who I was; where I could use my God given talents. I knew I was walking with Him. I gave Him the glory and credit for the program's success.

Children in the Breakfast Program

After the article ran in the paper, I was encouraged to run for the Model City Council. The council was to live up to the name "Model City". We would receive government money and use it to build up our city and educate young people (and adults) to become models for a better society.

Anyone could run and be elected to this organization, and I ran to represent area one. People used voting machines, much like today. There were two men who ran against me; men who had been involved with the PTA for years and who knew how to mediate and had learned how to 'play the game' and go along, do with (within reason) whatever was advocated. With my time working in school, I saw places where I thought that the money could be better spent.

Working and unemployed people needed to know of every resource available so they could learn to help themselves and become successful. During this time of Civil Rights, many people were afraid to speak out or didn't know how to make themselves heard without causing discontent. There were many who simply lived in fear. Period.

This was a time when there was lots of fighting going on and there were few places for young people to go that was respectable. There was basically no money for community improvements. The government came up with the idea of electing people from neighborhoods to serve as leaders and facilitate improvements. This program had money to offer blacks so that we could have so many things whites already had. We had been pushed out and not received anything for improvements.

While I had many supporting me there were others who tried to deter me saying no woman could do the job--I'd never have a chance. I was really apprehensive and a little nervous about running but I remembered (again) what Mrs. Lipham taught me concerning working to help people --- ALL people and to keep myself busy. I ran, with lots of help.

My campaign started. My opponents didn't work hard on their campaigns; thought they were shoe-ins. I asked Mr. McChanery, a teacher at school, if I could get his history students to help.

"Sure," he said. "That would be a hands-on learning experience for them but they can only work with you after school hours."

The students, some of their parents, and even some grandparents, came to my house and we worked and planned. They painted posters and worded fliers. Mr. McChanery had an idea to put ideas and slogans from history in my campaign. From his ideas, kids benefitted and learned how the voting process works. He came up with my slogan: What a better way to love your neighbor than to serve!

I thought—why not check out the radio and find out how much it would cost to have a spot there? I was surprised to learn I could speak FREE! and could announce on TV. We organized a parade. The newspapers and TV cameras came and covered the event. The students handed out fliers and marched. It was ironic that my opponents took advantage of the opportunity and followed along behind us, handing out their own fliers.

While all the planning was going on Mr. Field asked me how I thought the election would turn out.

"Well, I don't know," I said. "But I believe I can't lose because of the stuff I use." I meant the good people and Bible background and Godly platform.

I went to the polls and voted, then back home. A good friend came and sat with me that day, brought cake and we rested and waited. Then the phone rang and she answered. She turned and said, "You won!" and we grinned and settled back down. We'd never been a part of a winning campaign and didn't know anything else to do. The phone rang again and a loud voice boomed out, "Get yourself down here—you WON!"

Everybody got dressed up to help Mama run for office. New shoes, new (home sewn) outfits and ready for the parade!

This abused, motherless little girl—won!

I was twelve years old, scared and afraid when I left home to live with the Minnifields. It was hard to imagine how God had wrapped his hands around me and led me. God had always been with me and guided me and gave me wonderful people to help and support me. My campaign didn't cost me any money at all. And I was elected!

My long trip along governmental roads had begun. Little did I know just how far it would go.

Model Cities Group: This experience encouraged me to learn how to carry myself, conduct myself, around men. I have had a hard time knowing how to relate—probably due to my early childhood's abuse. I had to learn to respect and trust them. God led me in such wonderful ways!

Those of us who were elected were called together and sworn in. And so I became a member of our Neighborhood Model City Organization and was elected secretary. The school board, the city, and many other organizations were affected. This was part of the school's planning council. As a part of this Block Club, I was part of twenty-seven areas, including our block, who coordinated and worked together to build and strengthen our, as well as outlying, communities, and find ways to help people who were oppressed and needed help.

There were different areas that were addressed. It was set up like a wagon wheel: there were eight components, each component, like a spoke on the wheel, consisted of a different theme that applied to education: transportation, education, funding, housing, training, food services, health, and teaching. The council was the hub and worked with each area. I was put in the group to work in the education's and health committee's 'hubs'. We met monthly—in different areas of the state and even in different states, to discuss programs, go over our paperwork, and identify areas that needed help. Oh, so much to learn and carry back to the people! So much to do!

I am still in awe and amazement that I had the opportunity to start out with this grassroots program in our governmental affairs. So much has happened.
Many of these early programs died out and many grew and are still in existence. They changed and adapted to the needs of today.

I stayed in the breakfast program for a while after the election and was thankful to be able to travel as I needed to with the committee. I saved my sick and personal days so I would be free to go to meetings and training seminars. Little did I realize how involved I would become in these government programs and how much I would learn and be able to share with people over the years wherever I worked and lived. The knowledge of how our government works and the possibilities available were sometimes over-whelming. I enjoyed seeing new things, meeting new people, and traveling to new places as I participated in these wonderful, new programs being offered by the government. Surely, more people would take advantage of these opportunities—I meant to get back and tell everyone about them!

Because I was part of the education 'hub', I was even more involved in the workings of our school system. I recall being at school and learning of a black teacher who was giving one of the young girls trouble. The student was entering high school and came to class with an Afro hairstyle. That was looked down on by many people, especially by this teacher. She thought the girl was overstepping her bounds; trying to stir up (more) trouble. Civil Rights' demonstrations and ideology were blossoming everywhere, and many people wanted to avoid the dissention.

I knew this girl they were trying to discipline for something as simple as a hair style – her right to self-express. This young lady worked with me in the breakfast program and was a good, smart girl. I believed, like she, that she was expressing her right to 'be herself' and bring notice to many hurtful things being done to the young black community. The teacher took the student's Afro style a step further and accused her of trying to be high-and-mighty and advocate Black Power. The teacher came to my kitchen where the girl and I were working and blessed her out—right in front of everyone—going to far as accusing the student of being 'a disgrace to our race'. I was more than angry! I believed it wasn't the girl at fault, it was that teacher. Strangely, the white teachers seemed to accept changes better than the black ones!

Her Afro caused an uproar. The next council meeting some of the members were all upset about the Afro and wanted to ban the style from school. During the discussion a group of us walked in---all sporting Afros! Our point was made, and taken. The girl and others kept their right to quietly express their pride in their heritage.

Another time I went into a bad, poor neighborhood where many prostitutes worked to look around and see where improvements could be made. I remember getting a delicious baloney sandwich from a street vendor and eating it as I walked along the sidewalk: that baloney was cut thick and marinated in a special barbecue sauce and was the best I'd ever had. While I walked, I looked and listened. I was seeking ways to help these people get money and bring themselves up, and find places where the money could be used to improve the area.

As I walked along, daydreaming about ideas to spruce up the neighborhood, I suddenly overheard a man talking to his friend. "Look at her, she's not a prostitute; better leave her alone." I realized I might not need to be in this neighborhood alone anymore. I knew that where ever I went God was with me, looking after me and protecting me, but He also intended for me to use good judgment and get help for myself when going in 'shady' places—or simply stay out of them!

While I worked at school with the council, I realized a need for girls who had babies and no father to help out. Too many had to drop out of school and became a part of the welfare system. I worked with the administration and we set up a Nursery program for girls with babies right there in the school. The girls brought their babies to school and came to the nursery to care for them during the times they were not in an instructional class. The young mothers didn't "play" during their breaks; they came to be with their babies. While they were in the nursery the girls were taught tips on how to care for their child and learned how to become a more responsible mother.

As in most schools when a student misbehaved he (or she) was expelled and missed their instructional classes. No way they would ever learn if they were out of class, I thought—and what kind of mischief could they get into on the streets? So instead of expelling those students and sending them home, I had them put in a room with me to replace their out-of-school time. We went over their lessons, and in addition, we talked about their role in the community, and jobs, and how they could help themselves and gain self-respect and confidence.

After their time of expulsion had ended they went back to their regular classrooms. They hadn't missed any classroom lessons and not gotten into trouble on the streets. They had a new "chance" and for the most part, they took it.

It was a really rewarding experience, and we grew lasting relationships with many of these students.

There was Jesse, one of the students I'd gotten to know. He had been doing so well; was set to graduate, never caused any trouble. One evening he came to me almost in tears. He explained that on their senior field trip to the lake, he and a bunch of kids were having fun, playing around, and had thrown some trash (a couple of paper plates) in the lake. They were caught. As punishment he would not be able to march in his graduation.

I knew he had worked so hard and had sacrificed to buy his class ring and everything needed for his graduation march and exercise procession. He was hurt so and I thought the punishment was too harsh. How could one event crush all his work? I prayed and went to the principal and spoke for Jesse. He got to march and accept his diploma.

As one of my many goals, when I was a child, I had had a dream of being a teacher. Thanks to the opportunity to be a part of the education hub, I taught! My dream came true!

Jesse brought out the lesson of forgiveness and humbleness.

Everyone knew there were bad people hanging out around schools. There was one man in particular called "Knick Knack". There were always people in the fringe of the schoolyard selling snacks, but this man sold glue to students so they could sniff it and get high. He had to go! I ran him off—and that was almost unheard of—a woman, no less, getting rid of a 'drug' dealer.

As a result, a new rule was put in place: if you're not enrolled in school, you can't hang out close by. Some nearby store keepers, sad to say, were about as bad as the junk dealers: they encouraged students to steal and bring in goods for resale. That had to stop. Lots of people knew what was going on but did nothing. I couldn't go into the stores and stop this, but I could report it to the police. I did and the stores were closed up tight!

Nearby, there was a playground without lights and it was well-known that ten and twelve year old children were already involved in vandalizing the area. They were on their way to a bad end. Somehow, I knew and believed, pride had to be brought into our schools and neighborhoods, and people had to stop turning a blind eye to our neighborhood's problems.

Me, being council member who was expected to improve things in school, fight slum landlords, and make sure city ordinances were kept. I went, God with me, and faced the people causing problems. I did not feel fear. What I saw, I tried to fix.

The playground got lights and the children had a place to play safely. The "glue pusher", along with other loiters, were gone; the bad teachers chastised and threatened with loss of their jobs if they did not conduct themselves respectfully, and local businesses began working closer with us.

Later, during integration, we marched: blacks and whites who lived in our neighborhood. We carried signs to say 'bury segregation' and we ended up throwing signs in a casket. There was a preacher there to preach the funeral. It was a time of unrest, and a time of fighting and hard times.

Because of my drive to better our living facilities and schools, part of the time there was a policeman to escort me through the neighborhood. I didn't mean to make enemies, but when anyone stands up for what is right and Godly, there are those who want to put them down. I thank God for being with me and protecting me and my family. And for those who walked with me and faced fear themselves.

During the Nixon administration more federal money became available. My work in the community and involvement in governmental programs grew. I simply went where I was needed and worked hard. I was recommended by our local club to become a part of the greater Model Cities and was appointed, rather than elected, to this organization by the government. Through this, different organizations could apply for federal money and grants to improve conditions and fight injustices in and around communities. A SCOPE organization, centered in Georgia, provided money and our club applied.

Rosenberg, who was the head of the SCOPE program in Georgia, came to Dayton as a regional speaker, and I heard him speak and met him. He told of people not getting the money they were supposed to get through many of the new programs being offered. I'll never forget asking: How can poor people cook if they don't have anything to put in the pot? They needed to get the support and finances that were available and someone must check to be sure funding came through.

During that time many people couldn't get any money. Even many cities and communities missed their money that was allotted to help change the environment. I learned that the helping system was set up for growth—it looked at long term and worked on five year allotments. Then at end of five years, major projects should be finished and people in the city, neighborhood, and community had places and projects to take advantage of that they'd never have had without the funding.

There was money already allotted for projects and waiting to be claimed. All the cities and communities had to do was apply for it, use it for good, and reapply for final completion.

We learned that sometimes the money was used for

something rather than what it was requested for but if that happened, it had to be repaid. There were strict guidelines and the funding must be spent for what it was given.

It was noticed by some in our council that there was money available, but not being applied for, that we could use. The Model City Program was formed by the 'higher-ups'—mainly men. Women were secretaries.

At some point, we—members of the council and women included--- wanted to write a proposal and so there were white men who came in to help. Model City money wasn't only for blacks, but for all the 'have nots'. Some of these men, such as a lawyer, Roger Pritt, were not part of the council but saw the need and offered their help. The proposal was written, presented to the Ohio State Representatives and Senate, and was accepted.

When our application for Model City money came up the government officials asked how we blacks (in the council) would know how to spend millions of dollars under a Model City Program. The chairman of our committee block replied, "With that money, we are going to have a hell of a good time learning how to spend it!"

I suppose that wasn't the answer the government was looking for and that response prompted action that would insure the money was actually being spent for the betterment of the people. So at that point, we had to come up with a way to insure the money was well spent and accounted for to satisfy governmental requirements. We went to the city and asked for a contract to be drawn up to be sure that when we got money, however it was spent, it would apply to the city as well as to us and be put to the most benefit. This Equal Partnership between the city and the council was born and proved to be a smart move.

But it backfired on those who had been involved in previous SCOPE monies who wanted to squander it and take advantage of the program—sometimes bettering themselves. The city proved to be a watch dog. The money had to be spent wisely or be returned. An 'accidental' good thing!

I was the new member on the committee and had a lot to learn. Some of the others had been there a long time. I was excited to be a part of such a program and wanted to use the money for good. God led me again.

One project we used the money for was remodeling a new building and dedicated it the "Charles R. Drew" building. It was beautiful and became a vital part of the city. It was sad to realize that our work was not being recognized in the local papers---the whites' accomplishments were and we deserved to be written about too.

I was re-elected at the end of my term and was able to continue being a part of teaching and leading people to develop better places where they could enjoy their community and live better.

Part of our responsibility was to help people fight for jobs, seek equal rights in school, and be sure that everyone was treated right. Again, race wasn't a factor, it was back to the 'haves and have nots' who were affected.

Later, we changed the name of the organization from SCOPE to Community Action. Scope was phased out. People could get assistance for help with things as power bills, gas, and individual help that SCOPE did not offer.

Being part of this 'grass roots' organizing and forming the original Community Action Program was so rewarding. The program is still working in today's times and is helping people with different kinds of needs. It has changed over the years, and gladly so. Programs need to change with the times and meet the needs of people as our country grows. I realize how I have been a part of several 'grassroots' programs.

Not only Community Action, but later Meals on Wheels, and government funded daycare.

Not boasting, but I am so proud to have been a part of the beginnings of all this . . .

I felt that I was fortunate to be a member of the committee. There were many people who had fine jobs, others who said they didn't know how to set on a board or speak, and those who simply did not want to be involved. I couldn't understand why many who were so qualified wouldn't jump at this chance to help people!

I looked toward the big picture and thought of my election as a wonderful opportunity to reach out and help so many.

Part of my responsibility was to travel to different regions and meet with various groups to discuss how the money would be spent, if it was being used in the correct way, and how to help those receiving funding use it wisely. I was fortunate to be able to participate and have such a rich learning opportunity. My children were almost grown and they had learned to be almost self-sufficient, so I could be away from home for short periods without worry. A lot of my traveling was during school breaks or during the summer so I wouldn't miss any of my work at school. God worked a great scheme of things for me!

God gives each and every one gifts. It is up to us to find them and use them---or lose them!

Little did I know how far this beginning would carry me . . .

Twenty

Getting My Family on the Right Track

Next I find papers where my girls were in job training and my sons entered the job corps.
I think of the times we had to pull together to stay strong.

Since I was working for the school board and on the community council, when something new started in an area, I was called on to be present and pass on information about correctly setting it up. That meant travel to learn new skills and get necessary information to pass on to the working groups, as well as travel to and work in areas to teach others how to set up programs and grow. Lots of traveling!

It was about this time that my sons dropped out of high school. As it turned out Larry went to work and Eddie and Jimmy went into the job corps.

Eddie had gotten in a little trouble. One day he and some friends went to the movies during the specified time the whites only could go. They bought tickets and went on in. They were found out—someone complained about them being inside 'illegally' and a security guard came in and sprayed tear gas on them. Eddie ran out and kept on running, teary-eyed and knocking people left and right to get to the only place near enough where he could get water to wash his face and rinse his eyes: he ended up at the bus station's drinking water fountain. He tried to wash his eyes and stopped at the first one he came to. Unfortunately, he didn't use the 'proper' fountain—he used the one for whites only. There were police there and they went after him. He tried to fight them off but was arrested.

I got a call at work. Because I had worked at school with many students who were often in trouble and had gone to court to bat for them, I knew the judge. I called him and got Eddie home on probation under my supervision. His decision to go ahead and join the job corps proved to be a blessing.

Freddie, too, had trouble when he was about twelve. He couldn't lose his 'southern accent' and was bullied and made fun of in school. It was a torment to him. Fellow students accused him of silly things because he was the new kid from the south--such as his family not having real toilets down south and they found all sorts of taunts to set themselves up to be better than him and belittle him. Sadly, even some teachers got involved. It's hard to imagine adults treating a twelve year old in such a way, but it happened.

Freddie ended up fighting on the playground, and the school called the police and the children involved were picked up. The judge talked to Freddie, then to me. He went so far as call in teachers and discussed the situation with them. He agreed that something was wrong at school with this happening. Freddie was sent home to me. Things never got totally right, but Freddie was able to attend school in a better atmosphere.

Tim was in was beginning his junior year and started skipping school and he went in the Navy. Again, a blessing.

The girls were no problem. Even in the seventh grade,

they worked in the Neighborhood Youth Counselor (a government program) in school and I was close by and active in their school. I was thankful that the high school counselor kept the girls in jobs and involved them different programs.

I always set boundaries for my children and pushed them to be proud of who they were and to work hard. They had a say in what they would do and how they chose to reach their goals.

Integration was hitting hard everywhere and times were scary. I knew my children and believed they would succeed. Even the boys who dropped out of school had to go into something useful and not get involved in a bad crowd or just bum around.

The Bible says to teach the children the way they should go and keep them close and care about them. Wilma Jean married and went on to college. Willa finished Pharmacy Tech training and then worked for Urban League. I am so proud of all my children, I think, as I replace my papers and head outside to weed the garden.

Twenty-one

Travel, Travel

Go ye therefore, and teach all nations... Teaching them to observe all things whatsoever I have commanded you; and, lo, I am with you always, even unto the end of the world.
Matthew 19-20

We who were on the committees went from city to city attending workshops and seminars to learn how to give back to the people and help educate them to better their communities. This was an unbelievably enriching time for me when we attended conventions and met with others. We traveled to Chicago, then to Washington to Labor Union meetings. When I went to this meeting, I went as half of a team. Each team had one non-professional to represent the 'downhome' community and one professional, who made sure everything that transpired was proper and accountable. I had a lawyer go with me to the Labor Union meeting. Because I was involved with cleaning up our local school, I spoke to the attendees during this trip. Then when other speakers finished their remarks, I asked questions to better understand what they were saying so that I could accurately pass on the information.

For me these were great learning experiences. During these conventions I learned that people, ordinary people, should, and could, be involved in what was going on around them. In these groups we came to realize that as citizens, we all need to bring understanding and more knowledge about what everyone believes and feels between economic and ethnic groups together. This idea became to be The Citizens' Participation and through it more and more people began taking an active part in working together in a peaceful way.

As I traveled, I was amazed at how much there was to learn and do. I was appalled when many of the committee members skipped meetings and went sightseeing or shopping. Then they were eager to party, drink, and dance the nights away. Not me. I was proud of my responsibilities and took my job seriously. Yet there were those who looked at me and wondered: How can this 'country woman'; a woman who was raised in the south, work and speak as she does? The answer: God works! All I've ever done is listen to Him and try to get out His Message.

Then I was off to Philadelphia in the latter part of the '60s and early '70s. This was a greater time of tragic unrest—a time of integration when school doors were barred and locked and riots erupted every day. A sad, bad time.

As representative of our committee, I participated as part of a cluster of teams. People from different backgrounds met to seek answers and pursue a working plan to promote a peaceful transition in racial relations. There was a non-educator (me), a foundation representative, and a Fordham University, New York, representative, among others. What if I was called on to speak? I wondered. That was a chilling thought. I came from the south and even through rigorous practice never became proficient in proper grammar. I got up enough courage to share my thoughts with a colleague. Her response was much the same as Mrs. Lipham's had been years earlier.

"So what?" I remember Mrs. Lipham saying, "Who does know exactly how to speak? There are people who share their message and they don't even know English! As long as you speak the truth and from your heart, your message will be heard."

They both were right, I realized. From then on I prayed that God would guide my words and give me the strength I needed to speak up. I wanted to share the message: God loves us! We may be poor; we may have limited opportunities but we can get along. We can work together—all races and cultures—and grow and build better communities and a stronger nation.

There were many meetings, seminars, workshops, and learning sessions to go to for this organization, and our local Council paid for my expenses and the Union reimbursed the Council. The time came when the Council didn't pay and I missed meetings. All I could do was continue working for the Council at home, as usual. After I'd missed two meetings, a member of the Union contacted our Council and inquired about me: was I ill? Had something happened and I was unable to attend?

I don't know what explanation was given to the Union but from then on my expenses were met. To be sure I was on time and ready for the meeting, the Union began sending my plane ticket, meal ticket, and hotel accommodations directly to me ahead of time. ---God taking care of me again!

I became more and more scared and apprehensive about travel during this changing, disturbing time in our society.

Integration was creating more widespread violence and my next trip was going to be located in an already known volatile situation. I was told I would have two men to travel with me. Lo and behold, both were white. In spite of my belief in peaceful relations and a solid background of working and dealing with whites, I was afraid. My mind raced with possibilities that could happen; they could do anything at all to me—I could easily simply 'disappear' and never be seen again. I didn't know these two men, what they might be up to (in their hearts) and how they might mistreat me. Imagine, me and two white men traveling together!

My fears were unfounded. They took care of me. One sat on one side of me and one on the other. They took away my fears of how it would appear and any retribution: one black woman with two white men. They were professionals and treated me professionally. They knew how the programs and welfare of our children were first and foremost in my heart.

The Bible says there is no black or white, Jew nor Greek .. . .

Those of us who were part of the education hub went to schools for meetings and met with people in the school systems. Our job was to work with curriculum to strengthen it. One idea we proposed that student teachers be put into the classrooms for a period of time before they graduated so they would gain valuable experience and have hands-on teaching opportunities. This was a new idea that was adopted. Teachers didn't like the idea, said there was a thrust trying to take their jobs away. Nevertheless, the idea became practice and was proved extremely successful. Many longtime teachers eventually came to enjoy the extra help in their classrooms and looked forward to having 'student teachers'.

One goal of the committees was to provide money to the

schools for field trips. Children in the city, or any community, should see, touch and feel things so they would relate to and remember the topic of study. It is much different to see the crack in the Liberty Bell rather than simply read about it.

During this time I was fortunate to visit the Science Center at Temple University. I met with professors and interacted and let them know how we, the poor inner-city people felt. It was good that they wanted to learn and know what 'common' people were going through. We hoped changes would come from this.

I traveled from Philadelphia to Denver, Colorado. Workshop after workshop, discussing and planning community projects.

Then to San Francisco, California.
While I was there, I flew to Berkeley in a helicopter and was in total awe. I looked down and saw so much water! We visited the Wels Fargo bank and had pictures made.

We went over the Golden Gate Bridge in a taxi on our return. This was quite an amazing experience. Helicopter ride, Golden Gate Bridge, and another 'best": there were open fish markets there where we could pick out our fish and it would be cleaned and cooked it right there in front of us.

Yes, another time God was teaching me a lesson—
He teaches us at all times, we only need to watch and remember and when the time comes, we have what we need to face and overcome more 'hard times'.

In California our meeting concerned Health. I was designated as a speaker there, and naturally nervous as a cat, but I swallowed my fears and stood in front of that great crowd and spoke with pride.

Rose was living in California at that time, and coincidentally, after I spoke, I met a woman at the convention who came to me because she recognized my name: Cooley. After we talked, the woman went back and asked Rose (also a Cooley) after their church service if she had sister. And it turned out to be—me!

There were more learning and teaching trips: Manhattan, and Brooklyn New York, and St. Louis Missouri. At that meeting in St. Louis, I was nominated and elected Secretary of the Teacher's Union. While I attended the convention in St. Louis, I saw the famous arch over the river. Imagine my astonishment when I learned Nick Russell, who sang "Everybody Needs somebody to Lean On" was in attendance. I heard him sing his hit, and it made my heart flutter and brought tears to my eyes. Such appropriate lyrics!

Oh how his song affected me.

In Phoenix, Arizona, I had the last speaking position in the program to over two-thousand people. Of course I was nervous and concerned about my summation of the previous messages. A woman, a higher-up convention member came to me and told me to speak not with my mouth but with my body and heart and my message would get through. I did, and my belief was shared. She encouraged me so. God used her to let me know that I was doing His will. I was filled with hopefulness and renewed determination to carry on.

I discovered that it wasn't unusual for me to find a famous or well-known person, black or white, on the same team, sitting at the same table with me. I met so many celebrities. We all worked together, no big me's or little you's, to bring about peace and better living conditions for all people.

Something stuck near the corner of the box. A plane ticket. How this brings back a memory.

Our Assistant Principal, the Education Facilitator, and me (a councilwoman) had traveled to Manhattan on TWA for a group meeting. The airline had warned us ahead of time that TWA might go on strike and provided us with United tickets as a precaution so that we were assured a return flight. The Assistant Principal took the tickets and put them away. We finished the convention and arrived back at the airport, ready to board our TWA flight home, only to discover TWA *was* on strike. What to do?

The Assistant Principal was in a tizzy and was frantic: we each had our tickets but no plane to board! All my comrades thought of was the strike and how to get home, but I remembered our tickets were not TWA but United---and tried to tell them but 'little ole me' was brushed off. The other two kept trying to get on TWA, badgering the TWA attendants and complaining about the situation—paying me no attention, the simple councilwoman.

Finally as the two stood there at the boarding lobby in a quandary, I walked up and handed my ticket to the lady at the United desk and walked onto the plane, leaving my mates standing there open-mouthed. Boy! Were they embarrassed. It was then that they, like I, realized that a true education not just from books or degrees but from all areas and includes a lot of common sense.

Later, one of these travel companions who was speaking at our church, remarked on the importance of working together with people from all backgrounds whether they have college educations or not. She shared our 'plane' story and reminded everyone to never turn their back on someone who was trying to help.

More meetings: Miami, Florida; Palm Beach, California where we visited Disney World, on to Tucson, Arizona and visiting there and seeing it was such a beautiful place.

Then it seemed the time came when we had to go into places where there was more discord and mounting unrest. Our society was changing—sometimes with unity and love, but often there was a lot of resentment that spilled over and became waves of destruction and caused a deeper gash between the blacks and whites. Often gashes, large and bloody, occurred between black factions, also. Hard times and ill feelings were not simply healed. Feelings between people conflicted. We knew total integration was coming. It would happen, and we had to be ready.

Then meetings in Washington D.C. Those were awful times and people were full of anger and sometimes violence erupted. With this came lots of burning, looting, blood and even death. Even then, a sense of humor was necessary: While in D.C. at a meeting during the Nixon administration one of the members remarked as he looked around our hotel room, "Well, I don't see any *Bugs* here in this hotel!"

I remember Detroit, Michigan. I heard Maynard Jackson's speech there. That was a scary time for me. Not just the unrest and racial marching, a more personal fear. I had to get on an elevator and to the very top floor to sleep. It was so high! That was a new experience to me.—that night I really prayed for God to keep me safe in that skyscraper hotel.

God is with us in our lows and in our highs. He is with us in low valleys and on high mountaintops.
We are never alone.

More trips, more speeches, more learning and sharing. Denver, Colorado: such a strange place—the climate was finicky: hot to cold so quickly!

Massachusetts: home of the Kennedys.

Miami Beach, Florida: our stay was in the President's suite.

My life traversed many presidents. I remember Roosevelt as President when I was a child. Even then he advocated putting people to work. Work and a paycheck help build character and self-respect. And I remember his yellow grits and white navy beans—they ate mighty good.

Wish I could find some of them yellow grits today!

President Reagan advised us to turn over every one of our dollars at least three times to help the economy and prevent bankruptcy. Good 'spending at home' advice.

President Bush talked about Georgia being a perfect place for Senior Citizens. He looked ahead and I learned that lesson from him. He had a vision of Georgia being a good place to settle and live in the 'Golden Years'. His idea of learning trades and getting experience in several areas to be prepared to work at different jobs in case one played out was a valuable one to me. Go where the jobs and money are, he advocated. Don't wait for the money to float down and land in your lap, go after it!

In many of the meetings where I was to speak, I summarized the teachings of Dr. King and kept one idea especially in mind. I think he pulled it from verses in the Bible and is as much a universal truth today as it was then: If you hate the one who hates you, then you're just as bad as they are.

My work was, and is, for black and white. Anyone who

needs a lifting up; a helping hand or better way. Culture and carrying on God's Blessings are like a blanket that covers everyone, not a select few. My work is to cover as many as I can.

So many places; memories, hotels; travels, threats...

In the very bottom of the second box, I find a tattered old Golden Book. It is 'The Three Little Pigs. I lean back in my chair and remember how I loved telling my children this story. Not simply because the evil wolf was destroyed in the end and the little pigs were safe, but for other reasons, too.

I wanted my children to relate to the third little pig; how he refused to take the easy way out and finish his job cheaply and quickly. He was patient and found sturdy, solid materials to build his house. He worked hard to build it and made it secure and safe. That way, the "devil" wolf could huff and puff all he wanted to and if we are as wise as the third little pig, we can be safe, too.

I wanted to motivate my children to do all they could to succeed and be safe; defeat the Devil. I had to impress upon them how to read not just by reciting words and sentences, but read to comprehend, understand, and use what they read. I wanted them to be strong, hard workers, and be fair to everyone.

I nod. I have good children who have God-given talents. I am a proud mother.

During this time of travel, learning, teaching, and advocating, my children were growing and learning, too. They supported me and I think they were (and are) proud of me. I could never have reached so many areas, dreamed so many dreams of betterment, worked so hard to improve our community, and meet our goals without them. My church family was supportive, too. God provides for those who work for Him.

Twenty–two

Putting What I'd Learned to Practice

I wake early and resume organizing the contents of my boxes. I begin my time this morning finishing up a box I'd already been working in. At the bottom is an old menu: I see the famous "Cooley Burger". I smile as I am reminded of the time I stepped out on faith once again.

I stayed in Dayton from 1963 until 1980—years and years of traveling all over the country while I worked at home. While I was involved in my committees and working to better communities, schools, and neighborhoods I had a moderate income and managed as long as I budgeted and planned my money. Still, I needed a steady income to support us year-round.

The pay I received for work in the school's breakfast program was adequate and a part of my wages was placed in in a separate savings account that built up for me to use later, if I needed it. During one summer, when I wasn't working in school, I took out as much of my money that was allowed and started a small sandwich shop there in town. It was take-out only and the working area was only about a ten by twelve feet space. The previous owner had only sold chips and drinks, but there was potential for more.

I installed a small counter-top stove and made cookies. We did bun sandwiches and hamburgers. We made a big steak burger that we called a "Cooley" burger.

During this time I was part of a committee learning about a federal program to help people like me starting up a new business, and I was able to take advantage of that. When I got things going program overseers visited and evaluated my operations. I'd been paying cash to my children to help work in the shop and it was suggested that I pay them a regular salary so they would have more of their social security when they became eligible. They also suggested I pay regular taxes to the state and federal government to establish better credit. I followed their suggestions and went to work.

When school started a new year and I returned to work there during the week, I worked the shop after school, on weekends, and on all holidays. It really started growing. Freddie helped out when I wasn't there.

I cooked peanut butter cookies from cake mixes and turned the vent on "high". That smell went all through the neighborhood. People came in and when the children bought cookies, they'd go home and bring back what change they could find to buy more. Their parents would come in and buy more cookies and soft ice cream. Word spread and I was selling lots of food.

We stayed busy. I really prospered there and was really working hard and steady.

This led to me growing into a diner with eighteen stools where people could sit and eat. A real estate man came in the sandwich shop and saw what was going on. We were hustling and the shop was booming. He had a great place in mind and thought it would be a good investment for me. The diner he had in mind had been in lots of different hands and hadn't made a profit. It was in a good location, so I took the risk and bought it. I kept the sandwich shop and let Freddie run it.

I opened my diner and had sandwiches but no soft ice cream like we had in the sandwich shop, but I did buy and serve ice cream dipped from tubs. I was counting on people continuing to support me—if I had the same good food that we served in the sandwich shop, they were sure to come.

My diner was called Coolie's Goodtime. There was a popular show on TV called "Goodtimes". It was about a black family: the parents, a son, J.J., and a daughter, Thelma. It was so uncanny that Jean resembled Thelma and Timothy looked so much like J.J. and he could act just like the character in the show. He could do "Dine-o-mite!" just like J.J. did on the show. We thought this was a good, catchy idea that would stick in people's minds and they'd come in. It did help!

Because I wasn't afraid to work hard and attempt new things, many people saw me as unusual—maybe a little different, even. I couldn't understand that. I had been brought up to work hard and treat all people fairly. The people I'd worked with treated me good and taught me to be diligent, trustworthy, and fair. There were lots of people there in 'the north' who couldn't understand how I could do what I did—especially me coming from 'the south'!

God was working strongly with and through me! The work was hard and the days were long, but I was happy and found so much satisfaction with the success my family was having. All this time I was still active in my committees and travels. I was busy, but I loved everything that filled my days.

Jean and Willa started working with me in the diner. They weren't afraid of hard work either. I used those "southern" skills and loved to be around people. All kinds of people: from all backgrounds and economic classes came in.

It seemed like everyone knew me. I knew I'd come in contact with a lot of people but when I thought about it, I was involved in the children's school, the breakfast program, night school, our eateries, people who were on committees with me, the newspaper had an article on our business, neighborhood friends and acquaintances, and our church family. That's a lot'ta folks, baby

While Freddie ran the sandwich shop, the girls and I ran the diner. I had a grill out front and would make a big burger plate called a "hotshot". I hired a waitress who cooked all my meat outside on a grill (good smells drifted all down the street) and we also had fried smoked sausage. In the back was a steam table where I served mashed potatoes, candied yams, and green beans. Each day we had a different menu and candied yams seemed to be on it every day. It was a favorite.

We had a good system. Out front, my 'cook' would take the order. She'd repeat the order out loud so I could hear since I was just inside with the steam table. By the time she'd dish up the meat and put the plate and ticket back in our adjoining window, I'd have it filled up in a jiffy. People were amazed that we could dish up their meal so quickly. I don't think many caught on that I was listening as my cook repeated the order!

We did breakfast, too. My outside cook would grill meat and I'd put on eggs, grits, hash browns, and whatever else they ordered. I had breakfast kept warm and served it all day. There were folks who worked odd hours and they loved this.

My food that I cooked came from a grocery store; I didn't have any deliveries from wholesale vendors. I went to the nearby store every night or morning and picked up what we needed. There was a meat packing house a few miles out, and I'd get meat there.

Even with all this going on, I took time and enjoyed having a CB radio in my station wagon. My CB name was 'Mama Goodtime'. There was a CB radio club and when I started home, truck drivers checked in with me to make sure I arrived home safely. When one of the drivers came into town, he'd make a 'train' of truckers and lead them right to the diner.

One day a parole officer came in for lunch. Business was really good and he looked the place over. He knew many who were incarcerated could better themselves and possibly stay out of trouble if they only had someone to support and encourage them, give them a working opportunity. He knew when some young men came up for parole nobody would be around to stand up for them. He approached me and we talked about their situation. I felt for these young people. I had come very close to being incarcerated myself and had been so grateful that I had been able to help my sons stay out of major trouble.

We agreed that when he had a good prospect, he'd contact me and I'd go to the parole board and sit in and be there for the parolee.

I learned that if a parolee had a job for a year, they could go back into society and many times, they 'found' themselves and made out okay—a great success story.

And so it was that the people who were recommended by their parole officer came to work for me. I made it clear that everyone had to work. I hired thirteen different men and women who were parolees over a three year period. I became so familiar around the jails and courthouse that I could go freely into the prisons. I eventually had the same privileges as the pastor and doctor.

When I walked through those doors, it was a terrible sound when those iron bars clanked shut behind me. It seemed to echo and vibrate through my whole body. I shivered and shook every time I went in. My heart broke for the young people who had committed minor crimes having to stay in there. I knew that experience could make or break them. I wanted those who wanted to better themselves to have the chance.

It was a miracle that I found a young woman in prison who was originally from Bowdon. I got her out and she was under my supervision. She lived with me until she got her own apartment. Then she had to meet with me twice a month and be sure she was doing what she should to stay out of prison. I was so grateful to have met her. She was one of my special success stories.

I really felt my work in the prisons and for parolees was where God wanted me to be. He said in the Word to go to prisons and help and stand by the people there. I never forgot what had happened to me back in Bowdon; shooting Clive. That experience made me see a different side of the judicial system. The Lord was what kept me from having to go to jail myself. I could have been the one wearing prison clothes and walking in circles outside for exercise. The Lord spared me, I know. That event had to happen in order for me to have greater compassion and empathy for inmates—especially those who may have been judged wrongly.

Jesus said, 'Even as the Son of man came not to be ministered unto, but to minister, and to give his life a ransom for many.' Matthew 20:28

Everywhere I've lived some young person has stayed with me; every job I've worked, there were young people who learned about business and management. Always, young people remembered and sent me personal messages. I thank God for the opportunities I've had to work with them, teach them, and help guide them on to a better way of life.

Love Lifted Me

To Mrs. Cooley, I shall always remember your nice, beautiful smile, I shall always remember you. All I ask is remembrance, too. Always, Cathy

Mrs. Cooley, the only woman at RHS who showed me a new and better outlook on life. Indeed you are very beautiful and intelligent woman. Remember the conversations we've had. Love Ya, Jesse

Mrs. Cooley, To a person to whom I have enjoyed talking to at lunch hour. I haven't known you long but I feel that I have found a friend, Good luck to you, RMA George

Twenty-three

Being the Boss

...Another menu. This one from the restaurant. The place where I met and fell in love with my new husband.

Having waitresses and kitchen workers at the diner wasn't without some problems—parolees or not. The girls who worked as waitresses had tips coming in, the workers in the back didn't. The ones in the kitchen were jealous and wanted me to make the waitresses share their tips. I refused. I told them they had to learn to do a job and budget what they had. Everyone kept what they earned. I explained that I paid the cooks more wages than the waitresses anyway and the wages were fair.

Another was when I paid on Fridays, some of my workers were dead money-broke on Monday. This was a problem—more for them than for me but I started paying on Mondays to help them learn more about managing their money. It seemed to help.

I wanted my business to be a respectable, good business, in addition to serving good food. It was funny to me that it was thought by some that we served beer—simply because the shop and diner were always so full of customers. Needless to say, we didn't serve alcohol.

I left the business in my workers' hands when I had to be out. I didn't want my place to become a 'hangout'. I refused to let the waitresses' boyfriends come and just lounge around and I expected everyone to follow the rules-- especially when I wasn't there.

I expected honesty. I knew how much money was in the till and expected that money, plus more, to be there when I came in. I told the workers that if they made a mistake ringing up the meals, to stop and mark it. I told them how it should be handled for my records. If they couldn't follow what I wanted, even my daughters, they would be reprimanded. My girls were employees when they were in the diner. I never fired anyone, but a few, including Jean, quit.

> *Now I pray to God that ye do no evil; not that we should appear approved, but that ye should do that which is honest... 2 Corinthians: 13:7*

Love Lifted Me

Good Folks enjoying a good meal at the restaurant.

Twenty-four

Gordon

I separate the contents of the box into two piles: one to keep and display, one to pack back into the box. I snap the top shut and move to another. Right on top is a faded marriage certificate.
I have found Gordon.

The years passed: the '60s ran into the '70s.

All during the years in Dayton there had been men in my life. Not any that filled my expectations for a husband, though. There was a couple that I got serious about but had second thoughts about making a commitment. For a while, I thought Pete might come back and we could work things out, all sorts of things. I didn't think of getting married very often. Even with my work and traveling, I tried my best to stay in church and keep God close.

With my relationships with men came guilt. I couldn't be with a man without my conscience rising up and that feeling wouldn't let me live in adultery. I taught Sunday School and was active in church activities. I couldn't be a Godly woman and conduct myself in ungodly ways. I felt that if I had a husband, Pappa Jim would have another son and be happy. I felt so much strength from Pete's daddy and had an allegiance to him to be strong and always do what is right and good. I started praying for a husband.

Many people I talked to about this feeling that I had concerning finding a husband laughed at me. I didn't understand their attitude: I prayed and expected God to send me someone good to love and share my life with. What was funny about that?

I was still working the diner on Main Street. Lots of good-looking men came—and went. Lots of truck drivers came in: I kept my CB radio buzzing as often as I could. One day a new driver came in for breakfast. He sat at a booth and chatted away with his buddies. He knew one of my employees so I could easily ask and discover this fine-looking man's name. I left the cash register and told one of the workers in the back that there was a handsome black man out front and I was going to find out who he was.

He came in again and we talked. We started dating in May and were married in June, 1978.

Gordon Sullivan not only stole my heart, he tucked it away and made me feel special. He gave me his heart, too, and I loved him dearly.

Our Wedding Day, June 23, 1978, Gordon, Me, and our pastor.

Alicia Baney and Ralph Favors, famous Nashville Gospel singers, sang at our wedding.

I'd never had a honeymoon before, so Gordon took me to Myrtle Beach, South Carolina. I loved it there. Before our trip, he'd told me about a strip of land called "The Black Pearl" where black people congregated and lived. He had a camper like home away from home and we camped out there in the boondocks. He recounted how that strip came to be known as "The Black Pearl".

According to what he said, there had been a swap of land along the beach between whites and blacks. At the time of the swap, it seemed fair. For many of the blacks who stayed on the beach at Black Pearl, there was no desire between them to seek out growth and improvements and the land sat and staled while the parcel that the whites received grew and prospered. There was less prosperity along the Black Pearl beach and it became less desirable and more and more run down.

I saw so much: people cooking outside, the beach, friendly people. I learned how to cook fish 'the beach' way. It was a special place to me.

When we got back to Dayton, we lived in Gordon's apartment and rented out my house. Gordon was away on trips often but while we were together it was a happy, glorious time.

Then I had an opportunity to step up my food services. A real-estate agent came in the diner and asked to discuss a good investment. He had a restaurant available in his listings in a nearby strip mall. It was a good location with lots of ride-by traffic. I was excited and apprehensive at the same time. This was a huge undertaking for me. Gordon made good money and was good to me. I thought all was well.

I got the restaurant! I managed to get it open. Finally.

Unknown to me, the previous owners had been in trouble with the health department and they covered the problem up, pasted and put 'Band-Aids' over things to make them look good before I bought it so I inherited that nightmare. The whole thing had to be extensively repaired.

It came time to set up our taxes and regular payments. I had a bookkeeper but Gordon had never filed taxes, just didn't believe in it. I thought it was important for him to file jointly with me to lower our taxes. Gordon was afraid that he would be in trouble, so I had to go on in that area as best I could without him. I kept the bookkeeper, but didn't hire a CPA.

When we got it ready to open, it was a special place.

There were tables and chairs, a kitchen, a large room for special reservations, and a little room where we set up a lottery machine. When people played the lottery, I got a part of the money. It was good money but the guilt came flooding in again. I couldn't be a good Christian and have gambling in my restaurant. It had to go.

One morning, Gordon was supposed to pick up meat from a packing company and bring it to the restaurant. He never showed up.

So he'd left.

He didn't take any furniture, simply left the apartment for me and only took his personal effects and mementos with him. He left a letter and wanted me to know he wasn't mad at me. His leaving had nothing to do with me.

In his young, formative days, his mother died and I think he was afraid that if he got too attached to someone, something bad would happen—like it did to his mother. He'd told me that after his mother died, he was one of the original hobos traveling around the country, jumping trains, and seeing new things on his own. Eventually, his sisters found him and he was sent to a boy's camp and pretty much raised there.

It was a hard time in that place. As he got older, he saw boys run away and he tried to escape but some older boys brought him back and he was beaten. There were Bible classes there and he found that he could slip out during the classes. He managed to escape and found his way to his sister's.

He was a problem child and into one thing or another, bounced from one thing to another and nobody ever understood him. When he was older he joined the army, but couldn't stay there either.

Things just crashed around me. The day he left, I learned that my father had died. About this time, too, the doctor told me that he'd detected cancer and I'd have to have a hysterectomy. Then taxes and my finances had backed up and they all came crashing down around me. Thankfully, I didn't have to close the restaurant. Tax people came and were willing to work with me. They showed me how to do my paperwork and get a CPA and not rely on a bookkeeper. (I didn't know about these fine printed rules; nobody ever told me about all the payments that had to be made by business owners. I thought I was doing everything by the book.) Together the tax auditors and I worked out an agreement. I needed to carry on but didn't have access to borrow money or get small business loans to stay afloat.

I never had the operation for the cancer. With all that was happening, I trusted God.

Seemed like this was meant to be. The cancer has never shown up again and even though I didn't have any money, I still felt successful because I had been able to provide for my family, guide parolees on to a better way, and help people in my community. I wondered: What wonderful things could people who had money accomplish if they worked with God and tried really hard?

Love Lifted Me

And I heard a voice from heaven saying unto me, Write, Blessed are the dead which die in the Lord form henceforth; Yea, saith the Spirit, that they may rest from their labours; and their works do follow them. Revelation 14: 13

Twenty-five

Searching

I closed the box and looked at the stack of papers and photos I'd chosen to display. I picked up the stack and moved it to by bedside table. There, sitting beside the lamp was a small shell. My mind played sweet scenario from Atlantic Beach where I was reunited with Gordon.

I wanted to find Gordon; to comfort him. Two years after I'd married the man of my dreams, I left Dayton and made my way to find him again-- in South Carolina.

The first time I'd ever been to The Black Pearl, I was on my honeymoon. Gordon and I stayed a week and he took me around to a lot of places. I had gotten familiar with the beach back then and when I arrived this second time, I wasn't a complete stranger to the layout. Back in Dayton, some of my employees in the restaurant were from the area and that helped.

Miraculously, I found Gordon! We stayed on the beach and talked decided to go back home to Dayton. Most people who knew us didn't know anything about our trouble. Outwardly, things seemed good, but my heart told me things were not going to work out. Sure enough, he had to go and run from his demons again.

We had bought a car and after he left I tried to get the car in my name but found that the title was in Fannie *and* Gordon, not Fannie *or* Gordon. This was learning experience, and I would never make that mistake again! I thought hard to think of how I could get in touch with him. I remembered a restaurant where I knew he visited a lot in South Carolina and I called. I'd found him. He said to send the forms and he would sign them for me so I would have a clear title to the car. He did.

After a lengthy absence, Gordon came back to me once again. We really tried to get back to where we were on our honeymoon but that time had passed. Too much time had passed; we knew we couldn't live together. This time it was a mutual understanding between us when he left. We both realized our marriage was over.

I found that Gordon had been a living double life. With his insecurities, he had women in different places. That broke my heart. As hard as it was for me, I think it was harder for him. He was hurt and I believe he truly cared for me, but the demons he had inside kept us from having a secure, loving relationship.

In spite of all, God was always in control, or I wouldn't have been able to get through this devastating time of my life.

Life is a journey. All roads are not smooth and straight. Many are filled with potholes and curves. The important thing is to not pull over to the side and stay in the ditch; but to follow the road and keep going to the end.

Twenty-six

And Another Door Closes

That chapter in my life closed. I came to realize that with everything: the sandwich shop, the diner, the restaurant, trouble with Gordon, keeping tabs on my children, tax problems, the church, my committee responsibilities, I had become a wreck. I "woke up" and realized how I had begun depending on pills to get up and keep going during the day and more pills to relax and go to sleep at night. I had to get myself back on track or all my work would be in vain. What kind of example was I for doing God's work with all that going on?

I closed the sandwich shop and diner and kept the restaurant in the shopping center. I was able to slow down, get myself together, and center my life around God once more. I was content to stay in Dayton and work my restaurant.

God had other plans.

In all appearances, and true to them, with so many people coming in and eating, the restaurant was a huge success. I was proud of it.

One afternoon a man who was interested in opening another restaurant for himself came by. He was impressed by the customer flow and good food that he saw in mine. He told me he was interested in owning a second eating establishment. He hardly hesitated when I offered him mine and he was happy to buy it---if we could work out something that satisfied us both. He was impressed with what was there: a potential lottery room, breakfast area, cookspace, an area for younger folks to sit and enjoy their meals, and large center area for tables and serving. There was also a room in back that could be set up for business people to reserve. Without a doubt, my restaurant suited a lot of needs.

He took over the restaurant and I turned my lease over to him. Little by little, God was taking me out from under so much pressure. I was becoming whole again.

One evening a preacher came by my house and told me that the Lord had spoken to him and that I needed to move to a smaller town. I wondered at his words and how his message fit the same as mine. Yet, there in Dayton, even after letting my time-consuming work at the shop, diner, and restaurant go, I still felt tons of pressure. I was still very active in my elected offices, being compelled to run for other offices, and I was still involved in committee travels. I was being pulled every which way.

There was a need in the south for people to benefit from the workshops and from things I'd learned. Both my girls were still in school and both were smart and had learned to live independently. My children got their own apartments and continued working at their jobs/school. The boys were set up with their jobs and careers. Freddie was my only son still at home and he was a hard worker and wanted to complete his education.

I felt that God had indeed spoken to the pastor, and I remembered the words spoken in Bowdon years before when I left for Dayton. Whispering, comforting words came back to me from the Holy Spirit: words of encouragement.

Where do You want me to go, God? You have to show

me. He showed me Myrtle Beach: Atlantic City and Black Pearl.

I got a bus ticket and set out. When I got on the bus, I had a suitcase and three-hundred dollars to my name.

Along the way I had to stop at Cincinnati. I stayed a short while with Gordon's sister, Sarah. I don't think she really wanted me to come by her house, but I knew if there was some way I could make it that far, she wouldn't turn me down. She said she didn't know exactly where Gordon was but I suspected she knew his whereabouts, just didn't tell me. We both knew how his life was so sad and twisted and I continued praying for him.

We got her car and drove from Cincinnati to Spartanburg, and she stopped. I knew she didn't want me to go on to Atlantic Beach.

I suspected Gordon might be at the beach and I was determined to go on. I had to take the bus to Myrtle Beach, then a taxi to Atlantic Beach. In my heart, I hoped to find Gordon. I missed him. I loved him.

Twenty-seven

And Another Door Opens

*That ye might walk worthy of the Lord unto all
pleasing, being fruitful in every good work, and
increasing in the knowledge of God;
Strengthened with all might, according to his glorious
power, unto all patience and longsuffering with
joyfulness. Colossians 1:10-11*

When I got to Atlantic City, I got in the first taxi that stopped and asked the driver to take me to a nice, good place to stay.

He took me to a hotel called Skeeter. There was a restaurant there, too, and during the summer tourist months it was usually full. I arrived at the end of summer and many tourists had moved on to Myrtle Beach where there was more to offer. One of the first things I did was look for a church. There were people who said they'd never come to the beach to go to church but to have fun. There were people who simply didn't go to church in the summer; they were too busy! I needed my church and to serve God.

I ended up finding people who loved God but were

worshipping in a house. This was fine but we needed more; I needed more. I talked to the deacons about how I felt and they saw the need for a better building. We went to local businessmen, some who also attended services in the house, and together we planned a new worship center. The men tore down some of the walls in the house and replaced them with new ones. We built a new church around the house. We didn't have to spend a lot of money and start from scratch and build a new church but used what we had and made it better.

That reminds me of the condition many of us are in today. God can take us as we are and 'build' us up into new creatures so we are able to do great things. He makes us into what we are intended to be.

One day not long after I arrived, I was down on beach and was praying. While I was praying a vision of my mother came to me. In this vision she was telling me how in a lot of churches things were not right: men, even deacons, were going with married women, ungodly things were happening all across the beach. She was telling me there was a great work to do on Black Pearl Beach.

God had led that cab driver to the place I needed to be, in spite of its run-down condition. I began meeting new people and renewing contacts with some I'd met on my previous trips. I knew He'd answer my prayers and help me continue His work.

A few weeks passed and it seemed that my being here was a mistake. Things weren't happening that needed to be corrected. I felt so bad, so down, people were not listening to my message. This strip of beach was not integrated and was called Blackbird. I learned they had an association much like the one I was a part of in Dayton, but most of the blacks here would not attend meetings of the association.

Here was a job for me to do. I sent out letters and still people would not join in. I had a strong feeling that people did not like me because I was from Ohio (a 'northerner') and used that reason to stay away. I refused to give up. God had told me there was a need in Myrtle Beach and I refused to stick my head in the sand and give up.

I went to the association and began working for white and black—whoever was in need. Where ever I was, I could always see the 'haves' and 'have nots'. I went back out and spread invitations, and a few people started to listen to what I had to say. I knew that where two or three gathered together and worked according to His will, God would do great things. We had to learn to work together.

Through different organizations and government agencies, I learned that poverty hit everyone and everyone was entitled to the same help. Lots of people, including neighbors, and even people in the community called me Uncle Tom. White people were found in the 'have not' group the same as black people were. I didn't choose one race over the other. If someone needed help, I tried to get it for them. Many of the black community saw this as me being somewhat of a traitor.

I knew to treat all people, even those who were name-callers the same. I had to live love and peace to teach love and peace. I knew with all my heart that God had led me through my previous years of time and training so I could go into places and work to help bring about peace and betterment.

I had learned years before, when in Dayton and the druggies and thieves tried to be a threat, to not be afraid to say what I needed to, to be myself.

My little granddaughter, yet another of my angels, who came with her parents for a visit. When it was time for them to return to Dayton, she wanted to stay. She was a blessing and we learned to love each other even more during the few weeks she stayed with me 'on the beach'.

Not long after, God began working overtime in my life. Through His will and my contacts, it was planned that I would speak on the radio for black history. Again I went to God asking for words to ensure that this radio time would be used to the fullest. My words were heard. The newspaper picked up some information. The word was finally getting out!

I was contacted and received money from the local Art Council. That council was an organization to help bring people together from different backgrounds and use different avenues for them to learn and grown through each other.

Meanwhile, I had to make a living. I recalled while I was at that meeting in California that we visited the fish market. Vendors there cooked the fish right in front of the customer. Why, I wondered, couldn't I do the same here? There were many fish markets and I knew how to grill and flavor up most anything. So that's what I did.

That good grilling smoke drifted along the beach just like that grilled sausage drifted along Main Street in Dayton. People came. But there was one rule: no eating in bathing suits. There were ample places to change into clothes and cover up. Again, God provided.

I met a man who was part of the Art Association, and he told me about how art expenses could be used to fund association members to travel to different places to teach people about relations and help people find help and support they needed through various agencies. He helped me get elected onto the Art Council. Each member had to be elected to be on it and answer to the people.

Local State Candidate running for South Carolina Office participated in the parade. Encouragement! Encouragement! Encouragement!

From Dayton to Atlantic Beach there were those who encouraged me to run for office. This election was against two women: one with a master's degree from the University of South Carolina and the other a local property and business owner. I was re-elected and with a $250,000 grant from the government, we were able to hire and train more police and firemen, improve sanitation, beautify the community, demolish or repair abandoned buildings, and work with landowners to redevelop many projects.

This sharecropper's daughter-- and so called 'Black Horse' in the election-- who lived in rural Georgia and Alabama had come a long way, Baby!

I was able to continue to help people learn do things to better themselves. The council paid for tickets for me to travel. I could go to meetings by bus and fly and meet people all around once again. I tried to educate everybody wherever I went to learn about what was available and how to apply for help. They needed to know what blacks and whites were doing to try to get along and why it was important to love each other. Race relations were still bursting into flames all over the country. The message must be spread: love one another.

In so many places there were people spinning their wheels; living from day to day, paycheck to paycheck. At the bottom of the stack were the poor people who didn't have anything. There were no jobs and they had no way of making money. Times were bad.

After I was elected to the council, I became acquainted with a man who owned and operated hotels in the area. I saw prostitutes going in the rooms to some of those hotels. My heart broke when I realized what was going on.

One day I waited until I saw a girl leaving a room. I went to her and told her not to let anyone use her. I tried to tell all the girls not to give in to this lifestyle, to be proud of themselves and with help they could get out of this demeaning situation. It was a hard climb for any of them. Only a few made it to the top and left their profession for a better one.

The men who controlled the prostituted girls tried to scare me—talked about killing. What they didn't know was that I had already killed someone and wasn't afraid to stand up to them. I had confirmation from God that I was doing what He wanted me to.

There was a derelict, a poor man without a home or a place to wash his clothing or get good food. I went to him and talked with him. He hung around the hotel asking for handouts. In our later conversations, he told me a bird had flown by and pooped on his head. He cried and said he wasn't worth shit. God loved this poor man and I wanted to help. His self-confidence and faith in himself had long gone. He needed God in a mighty way. All he and I could do was keep on keepin' on.

One well-to-do man tried to get me to change *my* way of living—and he had a palladium where people came to dance and drink. All kinds of things went on there. I refused to go along with his lifestyle. God used my determination and my continuing disapproval to soften the man's heart and turn his way around. He had money, lots of it. He and his wife had built a new building and didn't know what to do with it. He heard about how I was using people in the community to further God's love, and we were able to work together to use the building to help the needy.

There was another hotel in the area that was used mainly for prostitution. To add to the ungodliness, the owner was a deacon and his wife was a preacher's daughter. The city and he were in a continuous fight over the property. The owners didn't provide upkeep on the building and the rooms weren't heated. Winter came and the cold swept through the rooms. To make matters worse, the power was cut off for nonpayment. One of the women who was staying there got so cold, she made a fire in a bucket and the motel caught fire and burned down.

I wanted to do whatever I could to help rebuild, but to build it and run it the way it should be. Working together, we finally agreed on how the building should be run and it was rebuilt. People coming to the beach to work noticed the new hotel and they reserved rooms. It was used in the proper way and became a successful business. Because it was more respected, it brought a healthy vein of income to the beach area.

I made sure there was a room there for the derelict I'd been talking to and helping along. He had been so beaten down and was so depressed.

He finally had a good room to live in, hot water and a warm bed. I even cooked for him and carried him his meals. Things began looking up for that man. It was a slow, slow go, but he managed to improve. As he bettered himself others stepped up and helped him, too.

So many factions came together we did the same 'revival' for several businesses in the area.

We showed poor people who qualified how to get food stamps, especially the prostitutes. Then we had to make sure they knew where stores were that would take the stamps.

I worked with many organizations to help feed and house people: all people. Many blacks called me 'Cracker Lover" because it made no difference to me who got help. I took in people--all people--and let them know they had to behave and clean their act if I kept working for them to get better.

Then there was The Blind Man who brought his dog in with him. He was a cantankerous old coot. He informed me that when I was caring for people and teaching them, I wasn't really a teacher but a nanny. I paid his accusations no attention and got him enrolled in blind school. God softened his heart so that he would let me take him to the bus stop every Sunday evening and he could attend school during the week. I would pick him up the following Saturday. I discovered he would start drinking when he was home and I went to work to help him stop this habit.

He could get drinks somehow, but I still tried to help him. He got so bad that after he became so dog-drunk, continually drinking, he would sic his dog on me, but the dog liked me better than he did that old man and the dog loved all over me instead of attacking.

Finally, I had to put the man in the hospital. He was so mad and upset with me, he told all sorts of lies: I beat him and mistreated him. Once during his tirades, he didn't realize I was there and I heard it all. I said nothing.

Later the nurses told him I was there. He realized the Black Lies he'd told.

There are a lot of people who are blind; they can't see. Maybe their eyes detect objects, but they're still spiritually blind. That's an awful thing. In our work for God, we must get people to 'see' like Moses.

Tell them about Jesus.

There were times I'd get disgusted. Get low, cry, and want to give up. In my lowest points, I knew all I had to do was get back to God! He was where he'd always been, with me. I was the one who strayed, and all I had to do was reach out to Him and He'd be close again.

Twenty-eight

Continuing the Work

I had run twice and was elected for Model City planning council while I was in Dayton. That's where I got my experience and training to take control and utilize "THINGS" in our community and turn things around for the good in Myrtle Beach. With program help our communities could benefit, gain new or 'reworked' areas, and the people would benefit. It was an honor and a duty to use what I'd learned to help improve living conditions around Myrtle Beach.

There were times we set out Palm trees at City Hall. I noticed there wasn't even a flag pole there to fly the American flag! I went to the mayor.

"What about a flag pole?" I asked. "This is City Hall, the center of our community. We need to show our pride and patriotism."

The mayor chewed on his lip a moment and said, "Well, if we had one there's nobody to put it up and take it down."

Whew! I thought. What an excuse. "How about the policemen or firemen here?" I asked.

Freddy was with me for a while then and he put up a flag

pole and got a flag. It flew beautifully and the police and fire departments seemed really proud to oversee it.

I was kept busy meeting with a group to get community schools back in order and growing with new projects. One of the most beneficial things we found to do was to take the old school buildings where money was being wasted and convert them into useful places where they would be used in the best interest of the community. Many could be used for teaching adults at night, as well as during the day, where people could earn trades and obtain training for other educational jobs. These classes were to be integrated so all people would benefit.

Top: Pastor Chesnutt and his wife and children.
Bottom: a group in front of a project completed for the revival of our beach

So many buildings were simply torn down—just mortar and bricks. Instead of considering how to transform, they destroyed, putting the needs of the people last.

There was one particular meeting with the local school superintendent, community members, a council of mainly whites and one black. The speaker was Dr. Arthur Thomas from Virginia. He brought it to our attention that there were many, many blacks put in the Special Education Programs, many who were bright children and qualified only because of their lack of parental or community support and instruction when they were young. And this man was put in there himself when he was in school. Yet he never let this placement in school stop him. Later he became our director of Central State Schools. He helped write curriculum and worked hard for the children. Just goes to show how far anyone can go and grow. . .

I was representing Model City Education (nine schools to work with) since I had been elected in Atlantic Beach to represent that area. We were sitting around the table beginning to work and a group, all white, busted in. They had their wrists bound in chains and long knives taped to their wrists with knives sticking out from their bound hands. None of the whites ran, but my group scattered.

I sat.

When I didn't get up and go the people who barged in looked at me with respect. This resulted in another meeting later on where there was an agenda and anyone could speak who followed decorum.

At that time, the group called Black Panthers became active in the area. They, too, saw the need for improvement. When a family needed money to pay their electric bill, or groceries, or clothing and shoes, they were there to provide help. Because I was committed to the same goals of community improvement and helping all those in need, we had something in common. They helped rid the area of drug dealers and folks who would cheat people. They'd just go in and clear them out. In those days, in the beginning, the Black Panthers provided much needed support of those needing food, clothing, and shelter. They didn't mind strong-handing the drug dealers, cheaters, and those who endangered children either. The Panthers proved to be a strong force that helped many families and helped our community remain safe.

A group of concerned members and citizens gathered together to go to a special meeting to try to get Dr. Thomas appointed as our director. There were Black Panthers and Republicans along with the rest of us. Rightfully they could have rifles and the Panthers carried theirs. I was in the group and was chosen to speak to let everyone know that we wanted Dr. Thomas to be our director. We wanted to get our plans heard!

Dr. Carl, the Superintendent of Schools, didn't want to give us the time of day and wanted us gone. When I was to go in and speak, Dr. Carl tried to shut the door in my face. I thrust my foot in the doorway and he couldn't shut the door, so he had to let us come in and speak. He listened and, thankfully, Dr. Thomas got the position.

The next meeting we had was at a service center where a larger group of people could gather. I was to speak there, but found it was a volatile situation: Black Panthers on one side and New Republicans on the other.

What I wanted to share was from the Bible but I knew that to say that outright was to be called a fanatic so God gave me His wisdom from the Bible. One of the Panthers stood and said, "She can speak," and I did.

The theme I wanted to share was one heavy on my heart. I spoke to the group saying that we would succeed only if we worked together toward a common goal. I explained about our partnership and how promises had been broken. It seemed that we were fighting everyone: administrators, teachers, and even the occasional parent (black and white both!). I had to get the truth across: How justice must come forth and people must work together.

At the closing of the meeting, one man looked as if I'd taken a shotgun to him. He became red in the face and just acted beside himself. His conscience was bothering him, is what I thought. What I'd said wasn't unkind or accusing, just the truth, and the truth hit him hard.

Sometimes, we don't get our own way and we must do what we can to keep the peace.

The Lord always put somebody in my life to protect me. Whatever we were doing, cleaning streets and empty lots with children during the summertime, speaking in meetings, traveling on busses, on planes, or walking through campuses during civil times, the Lord was with me.

I lay the Atlantic Beach papers in my lap and thought of one day at Miss Mildred Lipham's. Jean had gone with me and was playing with her daughter, Mary. Mary commented to Jean how one day maybe Jean's daughter would be working for her daughter. Miss Mildred was quick to admonish. "Listen Mary," she said. "There will come a time when it may be your daughter who works for Jean's daughter. Never think times will stay the same." And she got me to thinking, too. She was truly such a wise woman.

And there had come a day: this black woman stood in front of a white group to 'teach' them and help them understand how God's people should act toward one another and build together.

Another job I enjoyed and received so much satisfaction from was my work in Helping Hands. I had gotten my certification to drive vans and so part of my job was to make rounds driving the Helping Hands van. I'd drive out and pick up seniors who were able to come to the Center and eat and drive them home after. While the seniors ate lunch, I'd deliver more meals to shut-ins. Every day I made round trips of a hundred miles.

Those people appreciated me. They told me about other drivers who sat at the wheel and watched them stumble and struggle to board the van. Not me! I'd get up and do my part, helping them and encouraging them to get in and find a comfortable seat. It was busy every day—but I loved doing what Jesus always told us to do—help others. I knew if the seniors couldn't board the bus on their own, they weren't allowed to come to the center for food. I showed them how to hold on, to try hard, and many continued coming that might not have done so otherwise.

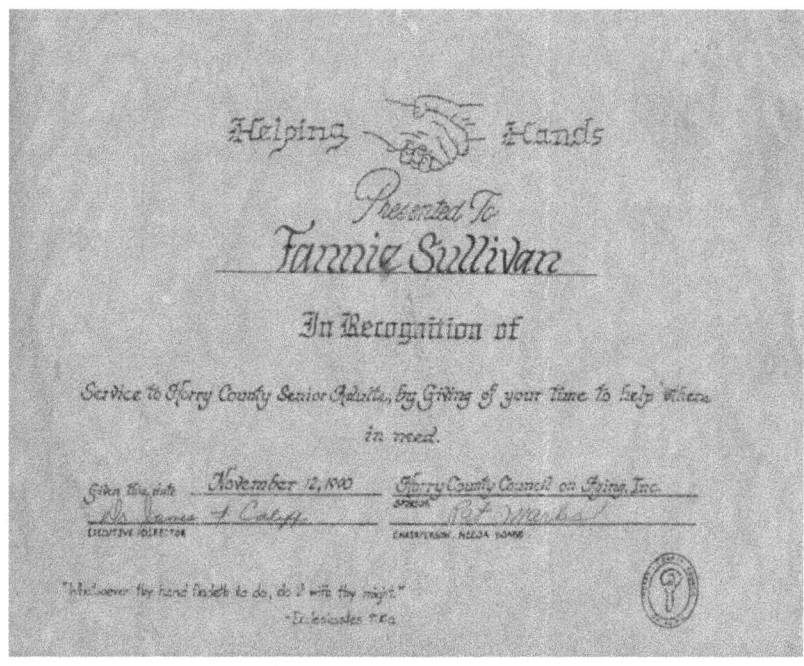

Twenty-nine

A Little Recognition Finally Comes to Atlantic Beach

Ah, I see a newspaper article about our Day Care. As I read over it, new memories flow…

While I was in Atlantic Beach, I saw an ad for a job in Myrtle Beach at a day care for three and four year olds. I was ready for a new job and applied and became employed at the local government funded day care center. Finally I'd have a steady income—and share my love of children, too. The staff director was from Africa and was the overseer of more than one center, and I was in placed in charge of this one. I was required to tape what transpired between the workers during our meeting's conversations so that the director would know what we had discussed and who said what. In the past when this hadn't been done, sometimes ideas got changed or mixed up when we were recounting with the director in a follow-up meeting, and by recording our conversations we kept the facts straight.

Each worker in the day care could have, should have, their CEA certificate, but I was the only worker who had obtained one. The workers thought they had experience and that was all they needed; they didn't need a certificate. What they didn't know was that the government programs required certain documentation in order to continue their funding and they had to follow those guidelines. The workers didn't understand this—just wanted to do as they always had. I had my certificate and my license to drive the day care bus. My job there was to use what I'd been taught in my Council trainings to set up programs, follow correct financial running of the facility, and implement the best curriculum for teaching the children.

One of the little girls who attended day care there had been burned. Her mother was ironing, and the little girl grabbed the iron and her hand was burned so badly. She ran to me when she came in that morning after the accident and showed me her hand. "Miss Fannie," she said, "my hand hurts."

"Let me see it," I said, and held her hand. "I'll talk the fire out of it."

The next day her parents came inside with her. I feared they were there to reprimand me—they'd never met me personally and knew little about me, only what the little girl shared about me with them.

They asked if I was Mrs. Sullivan. I held my breath and nodded 'yes'.

"We just wanted to thank you," they said. "Our little girl is just fine. We wanted to meet you and say our appreciation in person."

What a relief!

Day Care…What a joy!
Top Right: *The girl in white/pink had had her hand burned badly. I "talked the fire" out if it and she was fine!*
Below it and Left: COMMUNICATION SKILLS: *children share ideas and thoughts with a community person. They question about his job and he listens, responds, and gives good, positive feedback.*
Bottom Left: *children learn Patriotism, respect, and love for one another.*
Bottom Right: *The only little white boy in one of my classes. Color never mattered. There was a special connection between the child and me. When he had to move up to another group, he cried to stay with Miss Fannie.*

While I was at the day care center, I put to use what I'd learned during my Model City team meetings. We had white children in the day care along with the black children, but another day care that was predominately white had a beautiful playground. I wanted our children to have a beautiful, safe playtime where they could have a learning time, too.

I set up the playground like a fair using old tires and what equipment was already in place; see-saws and slides, swings and sand boxes. I made a choo-choo train out of wagons and a maze of half-buried tires for the children to crawl through. I gave out tickets for all the 'rides'. Children could earn tickets and turn them in for treats and snacks and in turn learned how to save and manage what they had. They loved the time playing there. The new playground was as big a hit with the parents and administrators as it was with the students.

Time came for the state social worker come and inspect our facility. She liked our 'fair' very much!

There was one little girl in particular, a little 'do things her own way' kind of little girl. One day she didn't follow directions very well, and I told her I just might spank her fanny. She looked right back at me, put her little hands on her hips, and replied, "And one day I might spank YOUR fanny!" In a flash, I realized what she said could be true. She could grow up, become a nurse, and have to care for me in my old age. Maybe I'd be somewhat obstinate and I just might need a spanking!

While I was at the center, different people from all walks of life were invited to come in and share their lives and occupations with the children. We had 'heroes' come in, like a local basketball player, someone from the newspaper, a well-known church worker, and public official.

We talked about how everyone had a little bit of each of the others within themselves: we all have Jesus!

We took field trips and brought in items to help children realize everything didn't come from the store. Apples come from trees, not the bin in the produce department, and explained how economics works to bring the apples from the orchards to the grocery store.

Later, as more state visits and reports were made, we were able to build a brand new building for the day care.

During my stay on the beach, I heard people fussing and complaining about not having money, especially for special occasions. I knew the answer! Help ourselves. God gives us the brains and strength to work for ourselves and not have to depend on others for the things we want. He provides for our needs but expects us to get up and work for our wants. I stayed to help and worked to create new businesses and help the older ones prosper. I worked with many who had money who was glad to donate and help out.

Fannie Billingsley Cooley Sullivan

With any job well done, there are rewards. Those rewards that come from the Spirit, Heart, and Soul are more precious than any given by man. During my time as a mentor, teacher, and business woman, I taught and shared what I had learned through the Council Government Developments and Consultations, Leadership Sessions, and Speaking Opportunities. Traveling and meeting in cities all over the United States was intimidating and sometimes scary, but what I gained and was able to share and teach as I worked was worth it.

Thirty

Another Day, Another Job

During my stay, working with the city and various organizations, Myrtle Beach changed. There were beauty contests and queens were crowned and proud to represent their areas. Drill teams were formed. We had parades to celebrate different occasions. There had never been a parade for Martin Luther King, Jr. Day, but we had the first one to celebrate and that began a tradition.

People learned how to get food stamps and where to shop in stores that accepted them. I helped them understand how the government provided programs to help them get on their feet—and then they should share that information and knowledge with others so they could better themselves. Help ourselves!

One particular motel owner was at the point of losing his property and reduced himself to letting prostitutes use the building—anything to make money, but it wasn't enough. He had to start renovations in order for the city not to take his motel from him. But help was on the way.

The Globetrotters had a house there on the beach near another hotel where we were working. They were famous and it was a treat to have them on Black Pearl.

A man from New York had rented the Globetrotter's

house and after talking with him, we got the Globe Trotters to come to perform as a fund raiser to help save the motel and help with other projects to save the community.

Harley Globetrotter James "Twiggy" Sanders.

Below:
  That's me in the middle of the group photo!

Later, was a man from New York, an alcoholic friend of the team, and when news about what good things were happening on the beach reached the players, they sent their alcoholic friend to come down to help get free of alcoholism.

It was wonderful working with so many different types of people and seeing how God can work so much good.

I stayed in Atlantic Beach and worked for twelve years. During most of that time, I knew where Gordon was. He remained in the back of my mind and I always missed him.

The day came when Gordon visited me, and I knew he had become very sick. I knew he'd never move from his home in Bennettsville and come live with me on the beach. I understood how he felt. He lost his mother and was brought up in a boy's home. He'd had a hard life.

About that time, I was approached and encouraged to run for another term on the City Council but I knew that God was leading me in another direction. I couldn't run for another term, just wait and see what road God was going to set me on this time.

Then Sarah, Gordon's sister, called and asked me to go to him. He needed help and she was unable to leave her home to care for him. She knew I loved him and was good to him.

And God intervened yet again. Gordon needed me to come to him.

Thirty-one

Facing the Real Deal – Racism

I ended up moving to Bennettsville, South Carolina, to take care of Gordon in February of 1991. He had become weaker after his cancer surgery, refusing any treatments, and yet still struggled to work every day.

There was a wonderful family living across the street from Gordon. They were Native Americans and good as could be. I came to love that young couple and their children. They were really good people and Gordon and I enjoyed having them so near.

They more than helped Gordon—they loved and cared for him. I learned more from them about Gordon than I'd ever known. They explained how Gordon helped people who needed help. He'd give people—black and white--- money to pay bills or to buy clothes and groceries. That made me think of Mr. Harvell back in Bowdon and how he gave what he had to help people—even me.

Gordon was a generous man. I'd known that he was generous to me but never known how he gave to others.

Gordon decided to buy a new mobile home and set it up for my birthday. We were together again. Gordon had a hard time having me around at first. He was skittish as a rabbit. I took it slowly and assured him that I was in with him for the long haul this time. He need not worry.

I remembered how he'd told me about losing his mother when he was very young; living in the harsh and unloving Boy's Camp all alone and living through the unhappy and disappointing experiences that he had. I cared for him and nursed him, reassured him that he could be himself and not worry. I would never judge him nor leave him.

He was scared after he had surgery—he refused any chemo treatments. He would never be the tall, strong man I had come to love, but I loved him still, and that was all that mattered.

We had a wonderful group of neighbors. They welcomed me and made me feel right at home. They had been so helpful to Gordon before I arrived: coming in and caring for him and seeing that he had everything he needed. I enjoyed their company and loved them just as much as Gordon did.

Good friends last a lifetime: Top right: wonderful Native American Family. Middle: Lew and Brenda

I knew I had to get a job, but for a few days we simply enjoyed each other and our new home. As we rode around the countryside, Gordon getting me familiar with the area, I noticed a plowed sweet potato field. It had recently rained and I spotted sweet potatoes shining in the field after the rain had washed off the dirt.

"What are those doing out there?" I asked. I'd never seen such before. "Why didn't the folks gather all the crop?" Seemed such a waste to me.

Gordon chuckled as he explained. "The owners leave part of the crop on purpose. Later today or tomorrow, soon as it's dry enough to get in the field, folks will come and gather potatoes to take home for their meals. Some even gather bushel baskets full and take them to sell. Farmers know how many people still are living in hard times and they leave a portion to help them out."

I understood. I thought of Boaz in the Bible who left gleanings of grain for the less fortunate to have. Ruth and her mother-in-law, Naomi, came and Boaz saw Ruth and fell in love with her. Such a beautiful story. Such a touching, thoughtful deed done by the farmers here.

At last I went to the unemployment office in Bennettsville with my resume. When the worker there read over my qualifications, he told me to get to the Senior Catering Service's office to apply for the supervision job *that day*. When I went in, they asked if I had any relatives working there. I didn't but did notice the name of a woman who had previously lived with Gordon written on some papers lying on the desk. She was coming in the next day.

I was disappointed to learn that the supervisory job had been taken by a young woman just shortly before I arrived at the job site. I had met a woman, Judy, when I had worked in Dayton and she knew about my work there and unknown to me, she had just been to the unemployment office, too. I'd missed out on the supervisor's position by a matter of short hours. It had already been given to someone else. It was given to Judy.

I went to work for the Senior Catering, which was a part of the Council on Aging Program, in a remodeled hospital. A woman, Judy, was over the entire aspects of the program. She knew that I had worked in Dayton, we had met briefly there, and like me, had knowledge about how businesses worked and had been active in organizing and setting them up.

Meals on Wheels needed a cook. I was hired to fill that position in the kitchen. I knew my experience would be an asset; I knew what was right and I intended to do everything I should

The Meals on Wheels section was located in the kitchen where meals were cooked, wrapped, and then put in trucks and drivers delivered the food. The lady whose job was overseeing the kitchen where I was to work was Sissy. She was younger and resented me from the start—thought I was a northerner who came in to take over.

I started the job, getting up and being on the road in the dark, the next day. It was demanding work and only paid minimum wage, but it was a job and I received a paycheck. Too many times I've heard, "You mean you work for minimum wage? Boy, I'd never take a job that paid that low!" I never minded—in my opinion, minimum wage was better than no wage.

The woman who had had a relationship with Gordon came in to work, too, and I was nice to her. She gave me lots of trouble, but she was not his wife, I was. She didn't stay long.

I found that the catering service provided about 1400 meals a day that went out to needy people. I had to be at work at three a.m. every morning. Sissy also supervised the packaging the food in serving pans, placing the meals in insulated coverings, and the deliveries. We had separate coolers to hold salads and desserts.

I realized fairly quickly that Sissy wasn't as familiar with the Program's guidelines as she should have been. I knew she felt threated by me: I had worked with the Council and had all kinds of training. I found out quick that the Seniors Program was running barely on a shirttail. I knew I couldn't begin changing operations without coming over as bossy and had no intentions of taking over, but I did, in a kind way, try to explain how to make things run smoother and more efficiently. My work with government programs had taught me how to set things up and keep accurate records and receipts.

It was here that a woman, Sarah Musselwhite first came to know me. She was the director that worked with the senior facilities where our meals went. She and I met, briefly, and she fell in with the rumors and gossip about me. Her opinion was quickly made concerning me…and not a good one.

As hard as I tried not to be, I was resented. I heard whispered comments: "How can she come in and tell us this? Somebody from the north has no business coming in and telling us what to do."

Judy, who was over the kitchen, tried to remain neutral. She tried hard, but sometimes she had a hard heart, too.

I felt totally exasperated at times at how my coworkers perceived me. I was a southerner, like them. I wasn't from the north, I'd just followed a road that led me through there. I vowed to stay on the job and make subtle changes when I could and not ruffle any feathers—especially Sissy's feathers. God had put me in governmental positions to go and learn—He intended for me to use what I'd learned to help anyone I could and remembering what I'd told Clive years before, I would be dead before not doing what God wanted me to.

After a couple of months the number of meals we needed to provide increased. Judy put me over the kitchen and moved Sissy over the office and supervising the truck drivers.

Sissy resented that I had earned a better position and I felt her animosity. She insisted that I punch in on the time clock like the other workers, but since Judy had put me over the kitchen I was on straight pay; I came in early lots of mornings and was allowed to take time off. Sissy really didn't like that! Not a black woman that should have those responsibilities. I stood my ground. Judy had put me in that position, and I did as she said I could. Judy was always good to me, but I know she felt that she had to walk on eggshells to stay out of trouble if she was kind to me.

Fannie Billingsley Cooley Sullivan

What we do is less than a drop in the ocean. But if that drop were missing, the ocean would lack something. ~ *Mother Teresa*

Thirty-two

Things Come to a Head

*He who dwells in the shelter of the Most High
Will rest in the shadow of the Almighty...
He will cover you with His feathers,
And under His wings you will find refuge.
Psalm 91: 1, 4* NIV

I learned that the people around there had never marched or celebrated one special holiday, Martin Luther King, Jr. Holiday. I asked around and talked it up so that plans were made, along with NAACP, and things came together so well that we had a parade to celebrate. People were given the day off anyway and we had fun getting together and celebrating.

When I got back to work, Tom, one of the workers, made the comment that somebody should have run over me while I was marching down the street. He came in the next day and banged his lunch tray down hard on the table where I was sitting and stared at me. I told him to look hard all he wanted but he'd better not touch. He knew not to mess with me after that but he was never fired or reprimanded for what he'd said or acted.

One of the other drivers, another racist, began spreading

the rumor that I liked to spread my love around and not just with men. He was intent on giving me a hard time, worse than Tom.

I wanted to cry. I knew there were hurtful people in this world and the taunting only got worse. I thought of my son and how he must have suffered at the hateful words he heard from those boys at school in Dayton. No wonder he wanted to fight!

One day I went in to check on the cooler where the salads and desserts were. Henry, one of the drivers, came in and knocked a crate of milk over and it fell on my shin. A knot popped up the size of a goose egg. He saw it and a look of horror came on his face. Maybe he was afraid he'd get fired since he'd hurt me with more than words.

I looked down at the lump on my leg and quickly slapped my hand over it. When I moved my hand away the lump was gone. Henry's eyes got huge! I thought of the time God's healing came through me when Jimmy was sick and when that little girl's burn pain was taken away. I knew God had taken that knot off my leg but Henry didn't. I think he decided I was a witch. At least, from then on he gave me a wide spread.

I gave a quiet chuckle as I recall the look on Henry's face. Strange, I think, how God works through His Mysterious Ways!

Thirty-three

My Last Chapter in South Carolina

Be joyful always; pray continually; give thanks in all circumstances, for this is God's will for you in Christ Jesus.   1 Thessalonians 5: 16-18 NIV

For seven years I was with Gordon in Bennettsville, working and living in a new home, the mobile home he'd bought for my birthday. We were together again. This was it, the dream I'd longed for. I planned to stay and be buried in South Carolina with Gordon. I purchased a plot for the two of us where we would be placed side-by-side.

My job with Senior Catering was a daily ordeal because of my co-workers' sentiments, and Gordon was so sick.

For a while he was able to continue work. He drove a van for Meals on Wheels and at times he would transport people to the doctor or take them on short trips. He tried to help everyone; he even worked the night before he died.

I worked and paid the taxes, Gordon and I worked together to keep the other bills paid and we got along wonderfully.

His sister, Sarah, had the deeds to the land where our

home sat. Gordon had contacted her to get the deeds changed but she continually put it off. She may have been the one to purposefully put off the signing. According to Gordon, he didn't get any part of his father's belongings when he died. Not a good fact to dwell on, I thought, and it spoke volumes about Sarah's character.

Gordon had a pet name for me. He always called me 'Kiddo'—never Fannie. Early one morning he left the bedroom where we were sleeping and made a pot of coffee and had a cup. He lay down on the sofa in the living room so he wouldn't disturb me. I was still asleep in the bedroom.

I heard him call, "Fannie!". That sent a warning streak of fear through me—he never called me by my name, only Kiddo. I jumped up and hurried to check on him. We kept some cash in the house to pay small bills and for emergencies. My first thought was, were there robbers in the house and he was trying to warn me?

When I saw him on the sofa, I was calmed some, and asked if he wanted any breakfast.

"No," he answered, "just had some coffee."

When I got closer, I knew, I could see, something was wrong. I went and felt his feet—they were ice cold.

"Do you want me to get you to the doctor?" I asked. "Call and ambulance?"

He didn't want me to but I called the ambulance anyway. I knew in my heart that Gordon was in trouble. The ambulance arrived, lights flashing, and the EMTs rushed in and started working on him. He was stabilized but I knew Gordon couldn't do for himself.

"Take him on," I said, and they put him in the ambulance. I followed in the car. As I followed, I watched the lights shine and could hear the ambulance wail. I was so afraid.

Suddenly the flashing lights stopped and the ambulance

pulled to the side of the road. I got out of my car and started toward the ambulance and they abruptly sped away. Maybe they had to stop and get his heart pumping again. I never found out why they stopped but I believe they had to do some life-saving procedure on him to keep his heart beating.

I finally reached the hospital and had to find a parking place. That took so much time!

I finally got inside and wanted to see him. "Not now," they said. "He needs an operation. Even with this procedure, he'll have only a 50/50 chance. Will you sign?"

I did. After I learned he was being prepared for surgery, I called his sister and daughter and told them what had happened. Then it was wait. . .and wait. . .and wait.

As I sat in the waiting room, anxious to hear how Gordon's condition was, the nurse came out and said the operation went well. They were getting him to a room, she said.

Before she was out of sight the doctor came. He looked tired and grim. He shook his head slowly and said, "I'm so sorry."

I knew.

Gordon didn't make it. He passed in December of 1994.

His sister, Sarah, arrived along shortly with his daughter. They wanted an autopsy. Since she had Gordon's insurance policy and there was money to pay for it, I thought it was a good idea and went along. I wanted to know why he died. We learned that he'd had a heart arrhythmia and it proved fatal.

During the following days, even while Gordon was laying for the viewing, he didn't look dead. I couldn't believe he was gone. We'd had such a long time as man and wife, yet such a short, happy time together.

I was left with the mobile home. Gordon had it on the land but his sister still had the deeds to the lot. She'd never gotten around to the transfer but I was sure she would be good enough so I could stay on there.

Was I in for shocks!

Attending his funeral his sister and daughter were there, naturally. There was an old live-in girlfriend who showed up too, along with another woman who claimed to be Mrs. Sullivan! I discovered that Gordon had made an insurance policy out to both of them. It was a shock but I didn't dispute their claims for the money. I couldn't take anything that wasn't rightfully mine. I provided death certificates for them so they could receive their claims. I felt that Gordon had, in his way, tried to do right by them. He made sure I received a wife's portion of his income and in that way, he is still providing for me today. He was a good, fair man.

His funeral was a celebration of his life. Many of his friends were unable to attend the funeral. Afterwards, church friends, family, and neighbors came to our home and we had a wonderful, special service there: singing and praising God, recalling good stories about Gordon and enjoying the love he had shared with us all.

I thought of the days at the catering center—working hard and trying to care for Gordon.

The days at the center were hard, too:

I felt uncertain about my future but felt that I would be all right. My finances weren't completely unstable.

As long as I was still able to work at Senior Catering and get a social security check I thought I would be fine. I was able to work as a member of the Marvelle County Council. God was good to me!

Oh, but how I was to find out how just true it is that *vengeance is Evil.*

I took off five days during Gordon's death and returned to work. Conditions and attitudes from my workplace and coworkers only worsened. Sissy and the catering employees were not compassionate. The situation only got worse. I had to leave Senior Catering--- if not only for my peace of mind.

Again, it was time for me to move on. I quit and God led me to my own business venture again.

Thirty-four

Q and S

While I worked with Meals on Wheels part of my earnings was placed in a separate account that I could withdraw at a later time and use as I needed to. Left with no income and no job prospect, Gordon gone, and bills to pay, I went back to what I knew best: running a restaurant. Working with all the government agencies, learning how to set up and organize my paperwork, and experience in helping others get started, I knew that with all that 'learning' and my God's gift of cooking, a good eating place would be a hit.

Nearby in our community was an empty Pizza Hut close the school. I contacted the owner and we worked it out so that I could open a small restaurant there, but I needed help. I withdrew my savings from Meals on Wheels---all $500.00---and got to work. There was a kitchen already; greatly in need of lots of elbow grease, and room for some pool tables. I hired Willie Quick, a local man, to assist. He had ideas of opening as my partner, but it was too soon for that. He became my assistant manager and could work his way up.

Children today need to look to those adults who have overcome adversities and worked so that they became independent. Learn as they go; make mistakes, yes, but learn from them and build on them to do better. Miss Mildred always stressed that each person had to have that driving 'want' deep down in their hearts and that drive would help them be successful. She was right.

People needed to know how to do more that pick cotton and crop tobacco—those jobs would put food on the table, but not necessarily allow people to save some for the winter.

Willie and I came up with the name 'Q and S -- Fun Center for Children and Adults of All Ages!' for the restaurant. I thought allowing him to have his name first would help make him take more interest in our success. But there were problems with Willie from the start.

Oh, My! I flip through a folder and there they are! Fliers and another article!

The Fun Center Menu and review from a local paper

I put my foot down that our new place wouldn't be a 'hangout' or a 'joint'. There would be no loud talking and no profanity. Girls would sit on the stools or in seats in booths, not on the guy's laps. Willie was more of a 'big' talker. He was big with his good times, with women, and with his ego. He worked for a while but it was obvious that I'd have to let him go. He left and the work was harder, but at least customers had learned about our place and were regularly coming in.

As good as work and business seemed to be going, making money was hard. It seemed that it was getting close to another time when God intended for me to go in yet another direction. All I could do was hold on as best I could and wait it out.

About that time the Pizza Hut owner took the building back. He thought I'd stay and he would become the 'supervisor' over me and get a portion of my income, but Q and S had nothing to do with his owning the building. I rented from him—only. Then he offered to sell me the building, knowing full well that I could never afford it.

The owner of the Pizza Hut decided Q and S had lasted long enough. He auctioned the building and pocketed the money.

A new chapter in my life began. . . .instead of working with children in day care or in school, I started working closer with older people in an assisted living home. Sometimes it seemed that these lovely people had come full circle because many had become weak and somewhat helpless. They loved to be hugged and loved to listen to stories; and to tell stories too. Some needed to be fed and led by the hand when they walked. In many ways I was doing the same things I'd done in the day care.

I opened the kitchen attached to the Assisted Living's senior citizen's living area and called my new restaurant Fannie's Place.

Previously, seniors lived in one area of the building and had microwaves to use in their rooms and could heat their food, food that was delivered from my former workplace, Meals on Wheels, but so many people couldn't follow the directions and the food wasn't fit to eat. Some of the residents actually got sick! The microwaves were removed.

This facility was one where Ms. Sarah Musselwhite, who was in charge of much of the delivery from Meals on Wheels was involved, but with the seniors only. She knew of my dealings with Meals on Wheels and had a pre-formed attitude about me. Since she wasn't over the restaurant where I was, she had to leave me alone, but she watched me. She already didn't like me. I was to find out just how far racism can reach. It doesn't have to be only whites, or just blacks. Racism reaches its ugly tentacles everywhere and wraps them around anyone--- no matter their color.

People need to be wary and keep an open heart to ward away the cancerous racist tentacles.

At Fannie's Place, I had to pay rent and provide food for

most of the residents. All the bills that generated from the restaurant came through me; I had to keep everything paid. I had low prices, knowing the residents couldn't pay much—helping out as I could.

The residents in the center came in and ate first. I made sure all the residents got to eat and then the locals could come in. Some residents wanted to wait and 'visit' with the locals and fellowship with them but still wanted to be served first. I stuck to my guns and told them that they had to come in at their time or be served like everyone else.

A cousin of Willie's (from Q and S), Preston Williams, began coming in. He was wealthy from his real estate business. His mother had recently been released from the hospital and Preston was concerned because his mother refused to eat. He had done everything he could think of but she wouldn't budge—stubborn as a child! He thought if she came in and saw how much other people enjoyed the Center, she would perk up and get stronger.

As we sat and talked, she perked up. She started eating and her appetite took off! Preston was so appreciative.

Back at Q and S's Fun Center, I had machines where people could try to win money. I let the machine operators keep a few there in the restaurant and every so often they would come by and empty out the change. The only drawback to this plan was that when someone DID win, I had to pay them from my money I had and that put me in a financial bind most of the time. I told the machine owners to come pick the machines up. This financial predicament stayed with me well into Fannie's Place. I worked hard to make up the money and stay in the black.

Preston's wife couldn't drive. I had 'wheels'. Sometimes I would drive her to places where she could shop or just get out of the house. We became good friends. Preston learned about me having a hard time meeting my payments and offered to loan me money.

I borrowed money from Preston and always paid him back. I knew the banks charged interest, and offered to add that too, but Preston refused. He and his wife were good to me.

I was so thankful that God had sent someone like this family into my life. God didn't just drop them in on one of my clean plates but put them in place and I knew, through His teachings and reading the Bible, that if I did my part, worked for Him and shared His message, I would be taken care of. God does provide! All through this time I was working with our local church and they supported me graciously. Shiloh church (not my home church) in Bennettsville supported me greatly. They held special breakfasts and the men's group reserved spaces regularly. This group really supported blacks helping blacks. Without them, I don't know what I would have done.

Preston and his Mother, such an inspiration and help.

The director of the assisted living was required her to fill out papers explaining how the program operated, costs, and menus and send them in to the governmental agency that Governor Hunt's nephew was a part of. This agency funded the program. I gave her all our receipts and my records, and she used this. Our program was noticed and given special recognition for its efficiency and work record. We received a plaque for our outstanding management and nutritious menus. The director, because of her position, was invited to attend a banquet to celebrate our program's success. Unfortunately, her 'claim' to the management of the kitchen backfired. When asked to explain her kitchen procedures and how the success of the program came about, she was at a loss. She wasn't a part of the 'working' group and had to bring the plaque back to the center---with a long face. She knew Governor Hunt's nephew was wise enough to realize who the real person was who was responsible for the operation's success. I was so tired of all the lies and misrepresentations, but I needed my job.

Thirty-five

A Legacy to Gordon

Weeks raced along and the work at Fannie's Place was hard but lots of good came out of there, too. There was a Boy's Camp nearby supported by a local church. The boys came from all over: Chicago, Dayton, and South Carolina.

"It would be nice if the boys would come to church," I commented to Pastor Harrington.

"Sure would," he replied, "but the Boy's Camp is pretty strict with schedules. They serve dinner (midday meal) at 12 o'clock on the dot and close the dining hall as soon as the boys finish their meal. If the boys attend worship services, they can't get back to their barracks in time to eat. You know growing boys don't think they can miss a meal," he chuckled.

"There has to be a way," I said. I had some thinking to do.

That night as I finished up my prayers and had almost drifted off to sleep, God filled my mind with an idea. There wasn't a meal served on Sundays at my place but if I opened the restaurant and was able to cook up something quick, like hamburger steak, mashed potatoes, greens, green beans, and such, the boys could eat over there after church! I prayed about this and 'talked' about my idea with Gordon and with God. I knew Gordon had had a special place in his heart for the boys at the Boy's Camp and had always given all he could to help out there.

And that's what happened. I could buy Sunday dinner supplies fairly cheap and knew how to whip up a meal in a hurry. Not only the young men from camp came in but so did other church members after the young men were served. Good fellowship was enjoyed along with the good food.

When the boys first started attended services at church, they sat in the back. There had to be a supervisor from the camp sitting at each end of the church pew with the boys between. Still shy and awkward and unaccustomed to how to act in church, they held back. Gradually, with the help of the Holy Spirit, attitudes were affected. Both those of the boys and those of the church members. The Boys' Club young men moved up to the third bench!

It wasn't long, however, that with loving prompting and urging one or two joined the choir. Then two or three more! The pastor taught them how to pass the plates during collection time and some of the bolder ones became greeters, meeting everyone and shaking hands with the members as they came through the church doors.

Tears flood my eyes as I read 'It costs so little to teach a child to love, and so much to teach him to hate." The words written by Father Flanagan printed on the certificate the boys presented to me. They gave me the name of 'their Spiritual Mother'. I think of those boys and so many that went on to serve God in His service: music, pastors, leaders, and fine husbands and fathers.

Because of the work with the Camp and their participation in the church and our Sunday meals, I was made their Spiritual Mother, Director of Evangelism. I had to go through all the rules and regulations, training, and in time could evangelize. I went into Bennettsville and witnessed to people there and tried to help them and invited them to church—any church—to hear the Word of God.

Everywhere I've been, there had to be a 'home church' for me. My life cannot be coomplete without the help and guidance of God. Through His Word, I know that it is our duty to work for Him. We are not saved by our works, but are saved TO do good works . . .

As with the trials that so often came my way, trouble was brewing. Fannie's Place had become a success, yet I was barely making ends meet. All the bills came through me that were generated in the restaurant. I didn't charge much for meals, just tried to stay afloat and help out those who only had a little money to pay. The director wanted me to hire a certain girl, one of her friends, and I couldn't do that. I had all the help I needed and the cost would put me in more of a finacial bind.

I paid worker's insurance and it covered anyone who might get hurt or injured in some way in the restaurant. The center's director came up with the idea that I also have fire insurance and it should cover the entire building. Naturally, there was no way I could provide that and I wouldn't be able to purchase insurance for a building that I didn't own, anyway. This went on and came to no end. Eventually, we had to go to court to try to settle things.

The morning of the hearing, three Free Masons came in for breakfast. They heard about my troubles and offered to go to court with me. When we got to court, I was pleasantly surprised to see that I knew the judge! I still worked with the incarcarated as often as I could and he had seen me in court before—but under much different circumstances.

Hunt's nephew, the building owner, came too. He was unaware and very surprised about what was going on between my restaurant and the center's director. When the judge got down to finding out about the details of our disagreement, Hunt stood and acknowledged that he was unaware that the building director didn't cooperate and there was no fire insurance.

The end result was that the restaurant had to close. Mr. Hunt graciously offered me the director's job at the center but I was tired and simply needed to step away and find where God needed me to be.

As always, with every move, I needed the support from my church families.

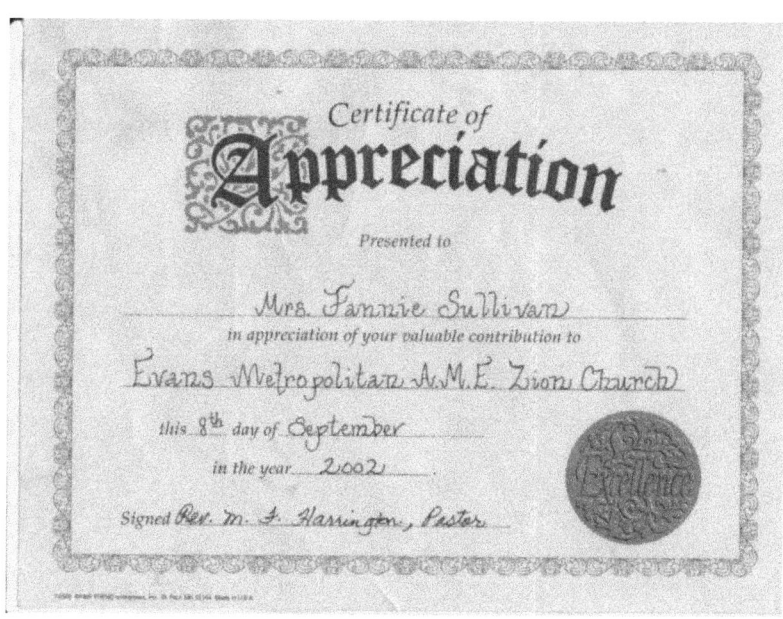

Thirty-six

Finding my Roots

But every house where Love abides
And Friendship is a guest,
Is surely home, and home sweet home,
For there the heart can rest. ~Henry Van Dyke

Gordon gone and buried. My 'home' in the mobile home unsettled. Gordon's sister scratching over my shoulder to try to get me to move the home off her land. Fannie's Place closed. Growing weary of the travel and work involved in the Council yet facing another year's service. I *was* tired.

Then—another setback. I was forced to move the trailer off the land. Gordon's sister had the deeds and she wanted me off. There were some kindly Latter Day Saints who offered me a renting spot but the timing couldn't be worked out for that offer: I had to be off Sarah's lots by a certain date and the lot owned by the Latter Day Saints could not be readied in time.

Eventually I did get the mobile home moved to a downtown lot and was able to live in it while the paperwork for the city was going through. Not live peacefully without harassment, however. Gordon's sister and daughter wanted me to pay off the debt left on the trailer and clear Gordon's things up. Naturally, that was impossible for me, I had no money, the weather was awful, and I had to wait for proper inspections and licensing for the trailer's permit to finalize.

I was tired, but still involved with the Bennettsville Council, zoning committee, the church, and helping people as I could. I tried staying at home, but there were still bills and I was on a very limited income. Too, I'd like to build up my Social Security a little before completely retiring.

At some point during all this turmoil, when I was at church I learned about an opening for a job at a local Senior Center. My church friends encouraged me to apply for the job. I did, and lo and behold, there was Sarah Musselwhite again. She sure didn't want me to work there, but she had to present every application to a board that had the final say in hiring. I got the job!

All this time, Sarah Musselwhite, (still over the Assisted Living meals) was filled with so much hatred. She was a very nasty woman and let her spite show every chance she could. She refused to let anyone say the words, 'Jesus' or 'God'. I learned that her son had been killed and she blamed God and never sought any forgiveness or comfort from Him. Still, her demeanor was something that was hard to work with.

One of the first things I noticed that the trucks drove in on bad paving that was covered in potholes and cracks. Musselwhite knew there were funds from the government that would pay for the repairs, but she wouldn't follow through on getting the necessary paperwork written up to present to the local board. That pavement repair was a job that needed doing—besides wear and tear on the trucks every day, the paved lot was an eyesore. Since I had been elected on the local council's board, during one of the meetings I made a presentation explaining the procedures and regulations to go through, and low and behold, the lot got fixed!

That was good for the center but bad for me. Sarah Musselwhite didn't like it at all that I'd 'gone over her head' and the parking lot was repaired. She was unaware that I was on the board and was doing my job in that capacity. Nevertheless, her jealousy grew. I didn't think that my work on the board and my work at the Assisted Living were connected—both had areas that needed to be fixed. Sarah thought otherwise.

I worked to make sure everything was done according to state and federal guidelines. People there weren't really resigned to the fact that a black woman, from the north, no less, could have knowledge of how the government wanted their programs run. My 'boss', Sarah, started giving me a harder time: a little here and a little there.

She said that I 'took over' and she wanted me out. I was only trying to help—not be a hindrance. She wanted me out. She hid and watched, accused, and spread rumors about me.

That was the point when Musselwhite wanted me to 'stay in my place' and in her opinion, I hadn't. She insisted that I eat my lunch standing up---even though all the other employees ate sitting! Finally I got so tired of that that I sat down, too Oh the hard looks that came then!

She said that I had to go to the doctor she recommended. 'Rules', she insisted, but I knew that doctor overcharged and gave her the difference; a nice kick-back so I continued using my regular doctor. She *really* didn't like that.

She'd write bad evaluations on me, but I refused to sign them because I knew what she wrote was vengeance, not the truth. Finally, when she discovered I owed some back taxes and had a garnishee on my pay, instead of taking out a minimum amount each month as she should have, she deducted the whole amount and fired me.

Since I was no longer employed at the center, I was eligible to go in and eat the meals like everyone else. That really set her off and she got a restraining order against me.

That was one battle I lost but in reality that woman lost more in that war than I did. I had God on my side and He gave me the ability to forgive Sarah. I've never forgotten and I've learned that people like her that are to be pitied more than hated. They have lost so much of their lives through hatred and it's sad to think of how much happiness, peace, and love they could have experienced and shared with others and their loving God if their feelings and attitudes had been different.

Hatred stirreth up strifes; but love covereth all sins.
Proverbs 10:12

In spite of hard work and dedication to my job, harassment followed. My work and training in sessions all across the country in governmental positions was put to the test.

> **NOTICE OF TRESPASS**
>
> Fannie Sullivan
> 1111 West Main St.
> Bennettsville, SC 29512
>
> December 1, 2003
>
> Dear: Ms. Sullivan
>
> With this letter I am putting you on notice that your presence at my home or at my place of business at the Marlboro County Council on Aging, on Market Street is unwanted and undesirable.
>
> **Any act in violation of this notice will be considered an act of trespass and you will be prosecuted.**
>
> Sara M. Musselwhite
> 215 E. Market St.
> Bennettsville, SC 29512
>
> Sign *Sara M. Musselwhite*
>
> Cc: 2
>
> Marlboro County Sheriff's Dept.
> Marlboro County Summary Court

Things had come to a head. I had to leave, just decide what to do. I had responsibilities to the city government of Bennettsville: my committees' term hadn't ended and I wanted to leave with a good name. I waited until my time was up, and I told my friends I was leaving.

So I gave up and let them have the whole thing.

Again, what to do? I should have never feared. God is always in control. By February, feeling so low, so lonely, and filled with all the trouble and heartache I'd been through, I was almost at the point of having a great big pity party for myself.

Then I got a phone call from Freddie, back in Bowdon. "We need you back home," he said.

Larry and the girls were still in Ohio, doing very well. They wanted me to return there and rest. Rest? ME?

Following their own roads, Eddie, Jimmy, Freddie, and Tim had settled back in Bowdon. Freddie was the most independent and never asked anything of me. He was the most like me, I think, wanting to help others and make his own way.

Jimmy owned land in Bowdon. If the city hadn't had an ordinance prohibiting setting up mobile homes within the city limits, I could have moved right on in.

I sighed as I held the slip of paper where the Van Dyke poem was written. How true his words are, I thought. Suddenly my body felt as tired as it had those years ago when I knew I must make another move. But there is strength in moving on, I realized. With each move, whether it is a physical move, emotional move, or political move, I grew and became stronger. Then I felt relief and release as I had in Bennettsville. I straightened my shoulders and laid the poem back in the shoebox where it had rested so many years. I was ready to move yet again.

What we do is less than a drop in the ocean. But if that drop were missing, the ocean would lack something. ~ *Mother Teresa*

Thirty-seven

Arriving in a Whirlwind

Jimmy owned a mobile home and planned for me to live there. My daughter-in-law was looking into public housing but I was apprehensive about my move to Bowdon—personal reasons. My name may have been changed to Sullivan and was no longer Cooley; I had furthered my education and achieved graduation; I was still (at heart) a strong believer and worker to help people utilize available governmental programs to better themselves; I was an accomplished businesswoman, and I remained active in local church.

But I had shot and killed Clive back there in Bowdon.

In my mind there would still be repercussions for the shooting. In reality time had passed and there were a lot less people in Bowdon who had first-hand knowledge of the event. The rumors still persisted and were whispered in surrounding counties as well as Carroll. To them I was still a Cooley and I thought about that a lot.

Even in Dayton my involvement with Clive's death had followed me. I remembered when Linda Grant, a good friend, was getting married. One of the men there called Linda's fiancé aside and asked if he was sure he wanted to marry into 'that family'. That family whose mother shot and killed her husband. Truth was, Pete was alive and well! How stories, whisperings, and innuendos grow and spread; like a bad disease. Thankfully, the young man paid no heed and Linda and he remained happily married.

During my time of worry and trepidation, my old familiar friend's words came to me yet once again: Mr. Lipham- 'Now Fannie, don't you do like lots of people do.'

I knew things were going on in the public housing that I didn't approve of and my faith that God would work things out for me would prevail.

During the chaos and confusion of dealing with Gordon's death and trying to make my home in Bennettsville, I learned that Jean's friend, Robert, was scheduled to preach his first sermon in Dayton. With Gordon's sister's plans to oust me, I knew I had to get to Bowdon straightaway but I just couldn't miss Robert's sermon. He was a likeable and good young man and we had spent many, many hours reading scriptures and talking about God. He was very special to me and I would be in Dayton to hear him preach or bust a gut!

So I got to Freddie's and dropped off my belongings, loaded up what I'd need for a few days in Dayton, and set off with the Georgia red dust left to settle behind me.

Even in my state of exhaustion, when I got back to Dayton, I was elated to hear Robert. Just to think! Here I was hearing the sermon from a young man whom I'd predicted would one day preach and serve God. What a Blessing!

God's mysteries are wonderful. I would have never thought that I would be physically able to travel from Bennettsville to Bowdon to Dayton and still have any energy at all. The glow of Robert's sermon stayed with me and sustained me all along the long road back to Bowdon. I had little time to worry about where I would live or how I would make a living. If we follow God's plan and work for Him, we need not fear.

When I arrived in Bowdon, I knew without a shadow of a doubt that I wouldn't live in the housing projects. Jimmy Watts, Bowdon's mayor and Dr. Watts's son, learned that I was 'coming home' and wanted me to be in the city and use what I'd garnered during my government trainings to aid the city. I went ahead and applied for housing but knew that wasn't the place for me.

Timmy and Terrance, my grandson, came up with the idea that they could buy the old home place (land) on 'The Hill' from Pete's nephew who now owned it and build a new house there. Pete could move in and we could take care of each other.

Whoa! Not a good idea to me. I would help Pete anyway I could; he was the father of my children but to live with him? Not.

I knew who I was and the things I could do and my desire was for my children to be able to do the same; have the same drive and desire to do their best.

I ended up living in Jimmy's mobile home back on The Hill. Seemed like I'd been on every spoke of that ole' wheel and was back at the spot on the rim where Pete and I had our first home. So much had happened and I wasn't nearly the same woman who had moved into that new shell home with her family decades before.

I wasn't the only thing that had changed; The Hill had too. The roads were littered and grown up. My yard was a bramble and the place was an overgrown jungle. Also, it followed that when an area gets run-down that many 'less desirable' people move in. I knew right away that there were people living there dealing with things less than lawful. I'd been in places similar before and worked to clean them up. I faced my new home as a gift. I knew underneath all that overgrown, tangled soil; soil stripped of the debris and trash left to rust and rot was a beautiful garden. Like lots of people,

I thought. So many people hide their love and beauty underneath a layer of ugliness that is there because of depression, lack of confidence, or separation from God. With lots of hard work, determination, and loving care, those people, like my land, can be renewed and become a testimony to God's love and promises.

I worked. I sweated and I got bone-tired. Little by little the ugly was stripped away. Loads of trash and weeds, old cars, and rotten limbs were carted away leaving clean, rich ground just waiting to be tilled, nurtured, and planted.

One day a local newspaper reporter came by – not to interview me – but a neighbor but the neighbor wasn't home. She noticed me outside, weeding and planting, caring for the flowers now blooming so beautifully where unsightliness had been. She walked over and ended up writing about me!

The article was featured in the local county paper along with several pictures. It still astounds me how God finds ways for me to spread His word. In my dreams I would have never thought that nasty piece of Hill would be a means for people to read about God and His love.

Working on the Hill.

Thirty-eight

Moving to Town

A young girl, Kathy, who lived in nearby Carrollton read the article—where does this woman live? She wondered.

She contacted me and was adamant that she visit. She made the short trip and I learned that she was a thirteen year user of Cocaine. The Healing on the Hill article struck a chord with her and as she visited, we talked. Her heart was softened as she listened. Through lots of hardships, struggles, and pain, she quit her Cocaine habit. She became involved in church and was saved.

I rode to her church the bus just to be at her birthday party and church service when she was baptized. What a testimony she gave! She continued going to church there and became as one of my daughters.

All the while I worked to clean up The Hill I looked for a house. I knew my time in the mobile home was only temporary, and eventually, a lovely home-like apartment opened up.

I moved into a log house right in town. During the time there I noticed a produce stand located in a large building right across the street. I bought vegetables and fruit from the produce man who worked hard in spite of his handicap. He was permanently confined to a wheelchair. Eventually the stress, economic distress, and a decline in his physical condition led to his closing his stand. An opportunity opening for me!

My home in Bowdon. I opened my 'People Helping People' ore right across the street from this home.

I talked with the store owner and told him about my idea of having a thrift-like store there. I had discussed it with my pastor: a place where people could come and buy household goods, furniture, clothing, or cute knick-knacks for a low price. I could use the money to help needy people and even give people who had no money items to help them get back on their feet. He didn't seem impressed, wouldn't commit one way or the other, so I left it to God to guide me.

I was able to rent the building and goods came in from all over. Kathy, my angel, came to help! She was involved with a group of young people like her who had been living a hard and sinful life and turned to the Lord. They all came and helped me set up, along with friends and family.

We decided to call the place "Fannie's Place, People Helping People". I loved my time there. People came in and bought all kinds of things. I was able to give things to people as they needed it. The more I gave, the more items came in, proving that you can't outgive God.

Grand Opening: Attended by The Misfits, Kathy's group, who helped move everything in, and Mr. Tom Mead. Also Carrollton church minister. I was saddened, but not defeated, that my personal church minister nor church members came. 'Miss Fannie's People Helping People' store right across the street from my home.

Sandra, a special friend who always took care of me.

Then the economy hit bottom and hard times came close behind. I couldn't afford to pay the rent, electric and heating bills, and had to close. That was a sad time for me. I had met wonderful people and enjoyed talking with them so much. I stayed on in the log home only a short while after that.

Moving again.

Thirty-nine

And Here I Am

I have finally come to understand that it is only in the silence that I can hear the story of my life and the voice of God talking to me through the telling of it. ~Peggy Benson

≈

I sit in the swing at the house beside the window with the red shutters and pull my sweater closer. The cool fall air is welcome after the wet spring and hot summer. The daffodils have gone and been replaced with tall yellow sunflowers. They sway in the cool fall breeze. The pecan tree is bending her arms, filled with bulky green husks wrapping their hard covers around the brown treasure.

My youngest grandson comes running up the walk and hops up the steps and lands with a bound on the porch.

"Can we go inside, Grandma?" he asks. "It's kinda cold out here."

I grin and pull myself from the swing. He grabs my hand with his little one and pulls me along. The door shuts softly behind us as we enter the house.

"Put your sweater here," I instruct. He sheds his sweater

and begins looking around.

My boxes are cleared away. My certificates are gathered together and my special photos are hung on my 'memory wall.' Already, my grandson stares in awe at them as he slowly walks down the hallway.

"Who is this, Grandma?" he asks as he spies one of the photos hanging on the wall and points his little finger toward it.

I smile and remember. I put my arm around the little one's shoulder and bend so he can hear my story. "That's the time I was in Washington, D.C.," I whisper.

Not The End. . .The new Beginning

From Cheryl: I think about how our lives begin like a box filled with loose, colorful puzzle pieces. Our parents, as well as those who love us, set the boundaries—create the edges of our life-puzzle.

As we grow, pieces of the puzzle come out of the box and find their places in the blank puzzle board.

Sometimes, it seems, pieces from other puzzles have been mixed in with ours inside the puzzle box, and when they're brought out—they don't fit! We have to toss them away and search again, often in frustration and impatience, for the right piece that fits that perfect spot to create our puzzle's form.

Some of the pieces are beautiful and fit perfectly—filling their space on the first try on the board. Others must be turned this way and that before they fit, but when they do, they are irreplaceable and add true harmony and completeness to the whole picture.

Only when the last piece is added can others see the completed work—we cannot, for that last piece has filled the last blank spot and our puzzle is finished. We can only work toward our finished puzzle being colorful, somewhat whimsical and a lovely tribute to God.

Once our puzzle is completed, it is one that will never be forgotten, for many pieces would have been copied and shared, and became treasured pieces incorporated in other's life-puzzles. Each piece represents a time; a story, and will be picked up and looked at, held with love and respect—even remembered with laughter.

As we use up our box of puzzle pieces, we should carefully choose which to toss and which to keep. Our life puzzle is our legacy, one to tuck away and be brought out on those occasions when comfort, inspiration, and an added bit of tenderness are needed. It is the heritage we leave our children and grandchildren: with love.

My Children: Larry, Wilma Jean, Willa, Eddie, James (Jimmy), Freddie, and Timothy
These are the children God has graciously given to me.
Genesis 33:5

And they are:

Larry: lives still in Dayton and is retired. He has three children (one deceased)

Wilma Jean: became a teacher, but with the coming of integration, decided to leave the pressures and went to work for Chrysler. She has always been a great homemaker and housewife. Her husband has passed. Her daughter is an accomplished cosmetologist and her son a successful barber. She had numerous grandchildren. She remains a great church worker and community helper.

Willa: Is now a single mom with four children and numerous grandchildren and several great-grandchildren who lives in Ohio. Willa lives in Atlanta and is employed by Home Depot.

Eddie: resides in Bowdon. He has two boys and several grandchildren. He is successful as a handyman and dedicated community helper.

James (Jimmy): resides and works in Bowdon and is divorced. He has five daughters and five sons with several grandchildren and great-grandchildren.

Freddie: is married to his wife, Charlene for thirty-one years. They live in Bowdon and are business owners. Freddie is very independent and is a hard worker. He and Charlene have four children: three sons and a daughter, all successful. Two of their sons attended GA Tech. They have grandchildren also.

Timothy (Timmy) the baby. Resides in Bowdon in his 'blended family'. He works for the bread company and is partially retired from Navy personnel. They have five children including two sets of twins.

All my children are successful, great in sports, and have many diverse and special talents. They are smart and hard workers and I am so very proud of them all.

God spared my family. Daddy and my brother were both in service and not hurt or killed. Timothy was in Desert Storm and lived to come home. I have nieces, nephews, and a grandson present in the armed forces. God is looking over them.

I have good health and a positive attitude of which I am thankful. Sometimes people say that I am a politician—and I think I have been, as God used me to do His will to learn and help others. Now politicians do as they are pressured to do, so I am no longer a politician, but a servant. As a servant, I strive to do the will of God and follow his teachings.

How good God is and how He has blessed me!

Fannie

Miss Fannie celebrated her 84th birthday February 1st, 2014 and resides in Bowdon, Georgia. She is surrounded by countless friends and most of her family. Some family still resides in Ohio, and others have settled in areas nearby.

Sandra and children and grandchildren in 2007

An important part of my family's history:

The McLemore House, built my mother's brother, now a museum in Williamson County, Tennessee where my grandmother lived and worked for the McLemore family. John Christmas McLemore, the primary slave owner, had two brothers, Sugar and Reuben, who owned plantations also. Many of the McLemore slaves escaped to freedom as they crossed the Alabama/Tennessee border. Harvey McLemore, a former slave built this house. It is the oldest remaining black residence in Franklin and stands as a monument to the accomplishments and traditions of the city's black community and a gift for future generations.

John Christmas McLemore as a young man. Most of his slaves took his last name as their own.

Presumed to be John, the slave master, and three of his slaves. The story is that the woman is his daughter by one of his female slaves. His white daughter, presumably, was very jealous of her.

The Stax Record Company was affiliated with the name McLemore.

*Album cover "McLemore Avenue"
by Booker T and the MGS.
recorded by Stax*

Thought to be Link and me.

Fannie Billingsley Cooley Sullivan

A Special Thank You At Christmas

I had a very special Christmas, but first, to the Almighty and Merciful God, thank you for sending your son, Jesus, to save and show us the way back to God the Father of all mankind, thank you for loving us so much.

This has been a wonderful Christmas for me. First I want to thank my seven wonderful children, thirty-six grandchildren, thirteen great-grandchildren, and one great-great-grandchild. May God bless and keep you in love while holding you in his hand, for if you stay in the Church, He will see you through. I would like to have been with you in person for Christmas, but my spirit was there with you.

To the Pee Dee Conference of the AME Zion Church and Evans Metropolitan AME Zion Church, (my church) family, may God bless and keep us all in peace. To my pastor, Rev. Dr. Otis C. Robinson and his wife, keep marching for God, for a change is going to come.

Friends in Atlantic Beach and Myrtle Beach, may love and peace be with you. To the friends of Dayton, Ohio, all my co-workers who helped me and my children, and to Bennettsville, may God's blessings be with you. To my friends in Georgia and Alabama, where I began, thank you for all you did to help me and my children. May God bless and keep you. I am still praying and thanking Him for his gift to us that we all may have a right to the tree of life.

To all the leaders of the government, peace and love be with you. I know so many of you and worked with you in the Model City Program in the sixties and seventies. It was a blessing to me.

To all of God's Leaders, hold on with all the things God has taught you and the love God gave you for His people, that they may see Him face to face one day.

To a very special friend, Willie Quick, whom sometime misunderstood, I thank you for standing by my side and helping me reach my dream with the new restaurant.

To every one, thank you for all the love you have given, also the help in making my dream come true and continue to grow. I love you and thank God for all of you. Thanking you for you love and support,

Fannie Cooley Sullivan
New Owner and Manager of Bennett Point Restaurant

A message of truth applies to today as well. . .

Thought to be my daddy's family.

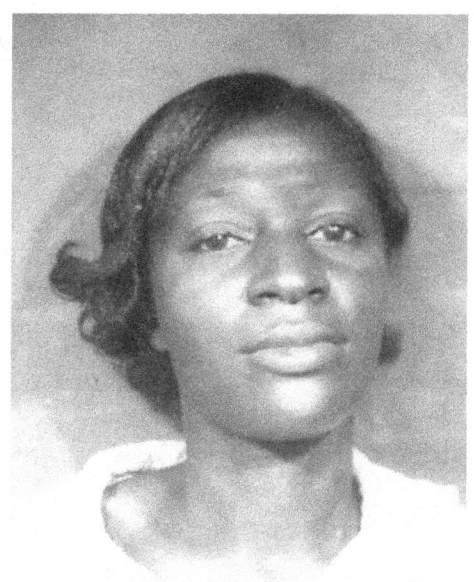

Possibly my daddy's sister.

Daddy's Father and Mother

Civitan Champions

Bowdon's 11-and-12 year old Team III won the A Division of the Civitan basketball tournament on February 13, 1992 by beating Mt. Zion. Team members: Sherard Montgomery, Maureese Nunn, Lee Gary, Matt Bristol, coaches Charlene and Freddie Cooley, Terrence Cooley, Jason Turner, Antonio Cooley, and Tobie Parker.

The champion team coached by Freddie and Charlene. They've always had a love for and dedication to the local sports teams.

Fannie Billingsley Cooley Sullivan

A special card made by a group of young athletes. Such a lovely surprise for me!

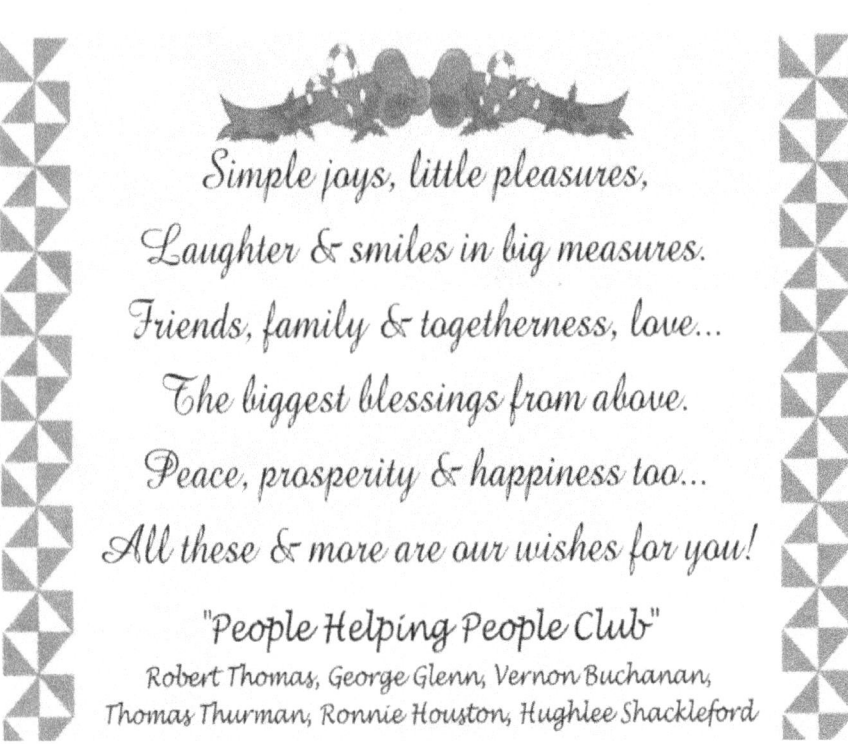

Love Lifted Me

One

One song can spark a moment,
One flower can wake the dream.
One tree can start a forest,
One bird can herald spring.

One smile begins a friendship,
One handclasp lifts a soul.
One star can guide a ship at sea,
One word can frame the goal.

One vote can change a nation,
One sunbeam lights a room
One candle wipe out darkness,
One laugh will conquer gloom.

One step must start each journey
One word must start each prayer.
One hope will raise our spirits'
One touch can show you care.

One voice can speak with wisdom.
One heart can know whats true.
One life can make the difference,
You see it's up to You!

Don't ever forget how very important You

Fannie Billingsley Cooley Sullivan

This and following pages: *Friends at the Bowdon Senior Citizens Center: These people have lifted me up and kept me in wonderful spirits.*

Dianne and Al Kasion

Fannie Billingsley Cooley Sullivan

Acknowledgements:

My family and friends—from all ages and all places

My church pastors and others:
- Rev. W. M. Willis: First pastor. He baptized me in a local Creek near Bowdon
- Rev. Joe Dunson: I moved to Flint Ridge Baptist with Pete when we married
- Rev. Wilder: Bowdon UMC, so helpful during the 'bad times'
- Rev. Joe Dunson's son, Rev. Walter Dunson: my church in Dayton
- Rev. Jasper Williams: a local radio and evangelist in Dayton
- Rev. Harrington: pastor in Bennettsville, associated with the Boy's Club
- Rev. Crenshaw : From Alabama and moved to Bennettsville UMC
- Also Rev. Joseph Johnson: along with
- Rev. Crenshaw, a blessing to me
- Rev. Mac Murdock, financial blessing to me, and
- Johnny and Jean Barr, who 'adopted' me

Photos are from the personal archives, albums, and collection of Fannie B. Cooley Sullivan

Quotes and sayings – Public Domain

The Holy Bible

About the author . . .

Cheryl Gore Pollard lives in rural Heard County, Georgia, with her husband, Jimmy. She is a retired educator and enjoys spending time with her seven grandchildren, painting, gardening, and making pottery.

Her writing style allows the reader to merge with the characters. Readers are somehow transported into the story and see and hear the characters as they tell their stories. Personal memories are recalled as the stories unfold, bringing meaning and inspiration that will fill the heart.

Mrs. Pollard is the international author of two books, *Fording* and *Sunrise* found on Amazon.com

Written and Illustrated
Cheryl Gore Pollard

Volume 1

Volume 2

www.ingramcontent.com/pod-product-compliance
Lightning Source LLC
Chambersburg PA
CBHW061942070426
42450CB00007BA/938